IT WORKS FOR US!

The Clergy's Church
Growth Handbook

BY MICHAEL B. BROWN

C.S.S. Publishing Co., Inc.
Lima, Ohio

IT WORKS FOR US!

Copyright © 1993 by
The C.S.S. Publishing Company, Inc.
Lima, Ohio

Library of Congress Cataloging-in-Publication Data

Brown, Michael B., 1949-
    It works for us! : the clergy's church growth handbook / by Michael B. Brown
        108 p.   14 by 21.5 cm.
    Includes bibliographical references
    ISBN 1-55673-509-X
    1. Church growth. I. Title.
BV652.25.B76   1993
254'.5—dc20   92-39129
                                                  CIP

9301 / ISBN 1-55673-509-X

To: Carolyn
who encouraged the project
and exercised exceeding patience
while I followed her encouragement.

Table Of Contents

The Approach

After evangelism has been on a back burner for 30-plus years, the mainline Protestant Church is once again discovering that "evangelism" is a special word, that it has a role in the life of our churches, and that the role is vital.

Perhaps some will say the rediscovery of evangelism is a knee-jerk reaction to wide-scale membership decline, and there is some validity to that argument. Others will contend that the church simply reflects the contemporary trends of the society in which it exists (20 years of increasing conservatism thus translates into a societal posture toward reclaiming past values within the religious institution). Still others will say that at long last denominational leaders have been forced to listen to what their constituency has been saying for decades. Those plus other arguments all have validity. The bottom line is simply that, for whatever reason, the church has begun once again to look seriously at its responsibilities to be about the business of evangelism.

This manual for pastors will respond to the renewed interest in evangelism, church growth and revitalization by examining several tested tools and proven programs that help churches grow and make them stronger. This will not be an exercise in speculation. Rather, this will be prescriptive: diagnosing both weaknesses and needs within the local church and suggesting ways to positively address those topics.

When Leslie Weatherhead pastored City Temple Church in London, he maintained a particularly effective ministry to the entire community (both those within and beyond his church alone). Everyone knew (and loved) Dr. Weatherhead. Often in mid-morning he would walk to The Commons where (as he put it) "the old chaps would sit discussing their ailments." There he would listen as they speculated on what may or may not be the best course of treatment for various disorders. "I've heard this is good," one would say. "I have a friend who has

7

a friend who tried that,'' another would counter. Yet a third would chime in, ''My niece knows a nurse who works for a doctor, and she said that she said that he said . . .'' Dr. Weatherhead observed that he always felt like hugging the old fellow who would finally say: ''This is what worked for me!''[1] Much in that fashion, this work will focus on what has been proven successful in local churches that wanted to grow.

The reason you have this manual in your hands is that you hope yours can become a growing congregation (spiritually, numerically and otherwise). The question is ''How?'' This study has been prepared by a minister whose church increased its membership from 790 to 1,200-plus and its worship attendance from 340 to 650 in five years. The study is designed to help you and your church develop a positive, practical, biblically-based answer to the question: ''How can it happen for us?''

The Need For A Vital Ministry Of Evangelism

Whereas little of worth is accomplished by too much sackcloth or ashes, there is still the need to establish why evangelism is a legitimate concern in local church ministry in the '90s. Thus, at least a cursory glance at a sampling of church growth/attendance stats is of value to the pastor who would seek to diagnose why his church has experienced decline.

In many ways, what will be reported here has been something of a global phenomenon (especially among first world nations). Donald McGavran did a study in Finland, for example, in which he determined that whereas 96 percent of the Finnish people were officially Lutherans, less than five percent actually attended church on Sundays.[1] Of course, the concern of this particular work is more local than global. A similar survey conducted by McGavran in an American city of 30,000 citizens and 62 churches indicated that though 60-plus percent of the residents considered themselves to be people of faith, only around 5,000 actually bothered to attend church.[2]

Every mainline Protestant denomination in American has experienced a loss of membership over the past 20 years (with the exception of The Southern Baptist Church). The United Methodist Church, for example, declined from almost 13 million members to just under nine million in 22 years. During that same period of time, it averaged closing four churches per week for 15 consecutive years![3] The Presbyterian Church (USA) lost 27 percent of its membership during that same period (in the period 1971-75, for example, losing 354 members per day). The Christian Church (Disciples of Christ) declined by 33 percent. The United Church of Christ lost 13 percent. The Lutherans and Episcopalians lost less on a percentage basis, but still declined.[4] Conversely, during the approximate same period of time the Southern Baptist Convention grew by 15 percent, The Church of Jesus Christ of Latter Day Saints (Mormons) by 40 percent, the Assemblies of God by 71 percent, the Seventh Day Adventists by 34 percent and the Church of the Nazarene by 22 percent.[5]

In the mid-'80s, over 40 percent of our churches had no constituency or prospective member lists. Many (in fact, in some denominations, the majority) conducted no membership classes for youth. Most conducted none for adults (and often denominational publishing houses did not and still do not even provide literature designed to address that need). In the author's denomination, 38 percent of all local churches did not receive a single new individual annually by Profession of Faith, 67 percent received fewer than four new members per year, and 31 percent reported no baptisms whatsoever.[6] Those statistics were not unique to that denomination but reflect the overall performance of mainline Protestantism from the late '60s to the late '80s.

Now, while Rome was burning, mainline denominational offices consistently decreased percentage allotments to evangelism ministries (many by as much as 15 percent of annual per capita giving) as well as allotments to educational ministries. Specialized causes and caucuses became squeaking wheels that received considerable grease while the heartbeat ministries of the local church too frequently went unattended. Interpretations of how and what happened vary, of course, even including old stale arguments about "actual dollar figures." When we go into the closet to pray, however, most become honest enough to admit that the church for a season forsook "evangelism" for other issues, even as "Demas left Paul, in love with this present world (2 Timothy 4:10)."

In light of all that, the argument persists that no one should get overly worked up about numbers. "After all," say the detractors, "we are not in the numbers game. We are in the people game." An interesting observation is that many who present that argument are quite honest and confessional, and their local church statistics will support them. Those stats reveal a long term disinterest in the numbers game (if not an outright ignorance that such a game even exists).

Are numbers really so important? The Bible seems to think that they are. Jesus fed 5,000 on one occasion and 4,000 on another. Someone was taking count (Matthew 14:21). Three thousand people were baptized following Pentecost (Acts 2:41). Five thousand heard The Word and believed following Peter's sermon at the Gate called Beautiful (Acts 4:4). "And the Lord added to their number day by day those who were being saved (Acts 2:47)." The Bible plays the numbers game without apology because it knows that each number represents a living soul.

Will Willimon and Robert Wilson put it this way: "Numbers mean people and commitment."[7] Additionally, they also mean income and increased ministry. They mean more effective programming and heightened morale. They mean new souls brought into the family of Jesus Christ!

Are numbers really so important? By all means, let us be honest enough to say: "Yes!" Every number represents a person. And reaching persons for Christ is the fundamental mission of any and every local Christian congregation.

Some Biblical Foundations For Doing Evangelism

Though God's Word is rich with calls to and resources for the ministry of evangelism, four passages in particular have outstanding applicability within local church situations.

I — Ezekiel 37:1-14: This is what many bishops or pulpit committees would deem "a challenge." (Experienced clergy learn to tremble in their boots at the mention of such things as "challenges" or "sleeping giants.")

Three young boys were talking one afternoon on the school grounds. They were engaged in a heated argument over whose dad was the richest. The children were respectively sons of the local physician, the local banker and the local minister. The doctor's son argued: "My dad is by far the richest. He owns the hospital. Whenever anyone in town gets sick, they go there and he gets their money!" The banker's son countered: "My dad is richer than that. He owns the bank where your dad brings all his money from the hospital, and my dad gets to keep it!" Quickly the minister's son spoke up: "My dad owns hell." The other two boys were dumbfounded. At last one said: "That's impossible. No one owns hell." "Yes, he does!" the child insisted. "How do you know?" asked one of his playmates, to which the minister's child replied: "I know because I heard him tell Mommy last night that he went to see the bishop, and he gave it to him!"

Ezekiel must have felt much akin to that preacher who had been to see his bishop. If anyone had ever been assigned "a challenge," it was Ezekiel. "Ezekiel," the Lord said, "what do you see in this place to which I have called you?" And Ezekiel answered, "I see nothing but bones, and they are dry!" (Some clergy at this point feel an immediate kinship with Ezekiel; they, too, have served pastorates in that valley.) God said: "Preach to the bones!" Miracle of miracles, when Ezekiel did what God commanded, those bones began to rattle and rise and attach themselves one to another. Ezekiel kept preaching, and muscles and sinews appeared upon the bones. Then God "breathed from the four winds his breath upon the bones, and they stood up, an exceedingly great host . . . And God said to Israel: 'I will put my spirit within you, and you too shall live!' "

Evangelism is done (even in the most improbable places) because God calls the church to do it, and somehow we believe that God still has the power to "breathe breath upon the bones" and bring them back to life again. The requirements on the local church end are simply faithful (and often creative) responses to the call.

For example, a church in the deep south was located in an inner city. Most of its members had moved away, leaving behind only the poor, powerless and aged. They were slowly dying along with their once vital church. A new minister, however, came upon the scene, and he was more interested in baptisms than funerals. He was more interested in resurrections than burials. And thus he challenged the congregation to identify at least one specific strength that was still "marketable" to the community in which it resided. The church members were unanimous in their self-assessment: "We are old, poor, powerless and waiting to die," they told their minister quite frankly. But when pushed to identify one asset, they determined that at least their building was still in good repair. The upshot of the congregational meeting was that the building was offered to the local chapter of A.A.R.P. as a meeting site. Week by week on Tuesdays scores of elderly neighbors came in for food, socialization and educational programs regarding health and finances. The program proved sufficiently popular that a Thursday morning group was established. In time, some of the A.A.R.P. attendants began showing up on Sunday mornings. New faces translated into new energy and new hope. Children who had moved away began returning on special Sundays (Easter, Mothers' Day), and were excited to see something happening in the old home church again. Little by little some of those who had fled returned. Within a period of five years, the active participating membership had increased from 18 to just over 600. And it all began when a handful of church folks led by a visionary pastor decided to think faithfully and creatively. God can and does still breathe new life into dry bones when given the chance.

A similar story is told by an old, downtown congregation located not far from a major university campus. After years of declining membership and attendance, a creative Evangelism work team decided to scratch where people itch. It was announced that three services of worship would be held each Sunday. Most church members initially reacted with skepticism, if not outright ridicule. The 11 a.m. service was celebrated in a sanctuary barely half full. What was the need for additional services? The response was that varying tastes mandated varying approaches. Thus an 8:30 a.m. service was established for families. The liturgy, music and sermon themes dealt primarily with family matters. A 9:30 a.m. folk mass was established for college students. The traditional 11 a.m. service was maintained unchanged. And to the surprise of all, the two new services thrived, and the third (traditional) service increased in attendance as well.

God can still breathe new life into dry bones, given the chance. That is one reason we remain faithful to the ministry of evangelism.

II — The second biblical passage to note is Matthew 28:19: "Go ye into all the world, making disciples . . . !" Jesus did not say, "Go if you have time — if it fits your priorities for ministry — if it is convenient — or if your church's administrative organization approves." He simply said, "Go!"

John Ed Mathison (who pastors American Methodism's fastest growing church) makes the statement that "the last command of Christ should be the first concern of the church."[1] That statement seems a perfectly fitting logo for banners, evangelism emphases, revivals or local church visitation teams. Jesus said "Go" and really did not give us the option to refuse . . . not, that is, if we are serious about being his disciples.

III — The third special scriptural passage is 2 Corinthians 5:20: "Now we are ambassadors for Christ, God making his appeal through us." Ambassadors, of course, represent their governments to others. They "stand in" for their respective heads of state. In this passage, Paul identifies Christians as those who represent Christ to the world.

In truth, the very word "Christian" confirms Paul's notion (literally meaning "One who is like Christ"). Thus, when we enter the marketplace, classroom, civic club, neighborhood, dorm, home or wherever we encounter others, we are representing Christ to the world.

Naturally, if a local church is cold, cliquish or clannish, it misrepresents Jesus, and the world looking on misinterprets Christianity. "Why should I go to church to be rejected? There's plenty of that to be found anywhere." Conversely, if the family of Christ is anything at all, it is inclusive, loving, caring, sensitive, open, embracing and warm. Those are the things Christ's ambassadors are called to represent to the world. If a church takes that call seriously, then it is inherently committed to the business of evangelism.

IV — In the fourth passage of note, Jesus disarms our oldest rationale for not reaching out to others. Every pastor is all too familiar with this argument when encouraging someone to serve on a visitation team. "Pastor, I'm rather private about my faith. I don't talk about it too well. It's so personal. I just try to live right and assume others will see that and know what I believe. But I don't think I would ever be able to go to somebody's house and talk about faith." Jesus said: "You shall receive power when the Holy Spirit has come upon you; and you shall be my witnesses in Jerusalem and Judea and Samaria and unto the ends of the earth (Acts 1:9)." In other words, much as God said to the reluctant Moses at the burning bush, "You will not be alone. I will be with you. Open your mouth, and I will speak through you."

The "It's too personal" response is somewhat confusing, given the fact that in other matters most are naturally eloquent and evangelical. Scout leaders often virtually "collar" people to convince them that life is best lived as a den leader. They are absolutely evangelical about it. Moms, dads and teachers get equally excited about the glories of P.T.A. and hit the saw-dust trail selling candy with passion. The quietest of persons can preach about the talents of his favorite basketball team. We all know someone who is forever seeking to win new converts to the Kiwanis or Garden Club. But, when it comes to Jesus those same people respond, "Religion is so personal. I don't want to be pushy. Anyway, I'm not very good at talking about it." In truth, what we say is not nearly so important as is the fact that we simply make contact with people. Herb Miller writes, "Evangelism is not so much a matter of saying the right things as it is a matter of making contact."[2] Furthermore, if the faith is important to us, Jesus says it isn't crucial whether or not we are personally eloquent because we don't go out to do evangelism alone. "You shall receive power when the Holy Spirit has come upon you, and (then) you shall be my witnesses . . . !"

These four biblical mandates inspire and inform the work of evangelism: 1. That God is able to breathe his breath into congregations, even those that appear to be as dead and life-less as was Ezekiel's; 2. That Christ calls and commands us to go; 3. That the world is looking to us as his representatives, and ambassadors for Christ who are not warm and evangelical are misrepresenting the gospel; and finally, 4. that he will be with us.

To this point in the manual, two ideas have been advanced. Let us re-state them briefly before moving on.

1 — That the need exists for a vital ministry of evangelism because mainline churches have been declining for more than 20 years. Declining churches are demoralized churches. Numbers are important because each number represents a human soul, and the Bible takes that seriously. New souls added to the family of a local church eradicate the prevailing ethos of defeat and despair and puts energy and enthusiasm back in their places.

2 — We have also noted that there are numerous biblical rationales for doing the work of evangelism, not the least of which are that we are divinely mandated to do so and live with the promise that when we say "Yes" to the mandate, Christ goes out to walk and work with us.

Prayer Power, Bible Power And Small Group Dynamics

Arthur Caliandro (Pastor of Marble Collegiate Church in New York City) made the rather bold public statement that, "No church can grow and remain vital over the long haul unless its people are serious about prayer."[1] Responsible Christians who are interested in revitalized churches add a quick "Amen" to his statement. If we want church growth, the best place to start is on our knees.

Some years ago in a lecture he delivered, the late Dr. Harry Denman said: "Prayer is essentially listening to God."[2] In his wonderful book *With Open Hands*, Henry Nouwen resonates with Dr. Denman's thesis that prayer positions us to receive what God wants to give. Unfortunately we are ordinarily so busy placing our orders, talking to God or about God, that we forget to be silent — to listen for "the still small voice" — and thus to receive what God has to offer.

Churches that are serious about growth and revitalization must start by listening to God — by asking in prayer: "What would you have us do? What would you have us be? To whom would you send us?" Having asked, they listen for God's reply.

Paula D'Arcy (the author of *Song For Sarah*) is an exceptional Christian motivator. She tells of belonging to a small church in New England. There were approximately 200 members on roll, with about 50 in church on any given Sunday. Usually there were about four in the choir. All was dull and dead: no new faces, no children, no laughter, no spirit to speak of. In time she and a friend began discussing the merits of looking for a new church home. However, they decided to remain until the end of the calendar year. In the autumn came the time for the annual women's banquet. Every year the same 12 or 15 ladies attended, nothing new, nothing inspiring. That particular year, though, Paula and her friend decided to experiment. They phoned every woman on the church roll and

19

asked, "Would you come next Thursday night? We know you have other obligations and don't ordinarily participate in this group, but just this once it's very important that you're here. Would you come?" On Thursday night, instead of the usual 12 or 15, 60 women attended. At the close of the dinner, Paula and her friend pointed out to those women a table near the door. On that table were 200 slips of white paper. On each slip was the name of a member of the church. Every person on the roll (whether active or inactive) had his or her name written on one of the pieces of paper. Paula said to the women, "On your way out, I want each of you to pick up three or four of these pieces of paper. Then, for the coming year, I just want to ask you to do one thing: Pray for the persons whose names you picked up. You don't have to talk to them, socialize with them or even like them. Just pray for them, that's all." The women responded positively (with Paula and her friend taking whatever slips of paper that remained on the table as their prayer projects). "At the end of six months," she said, "things were different in our church. The choir was better. The preaching was better (proving either that sermons grow stronger in response to prayer or that people become better listeners when they pray for the preacher). People weren't in such a rush to leave after worship. Attendance was up. Young families were beginning to bring their children back. Occasionally a new member would be received. Folks were smiling and chatting in the halls. After a year," she said, "my friend and I didn't have to go looking for a new church. We were in one!" It all happened simply because of the power of prayer. People began to relate to one another differently, to feel better about themselves and others, and that spilled over into the fabric of the entire church.[3]

Psychologically it has been proven to be impossible to hate someone for whom you are praying. This author made the statement some time ago in a sermon that if we pray seriously for another person every day for two weeks, no matter what sort of grudge we feel it will subside. A church member decided to put the statement to a test. Later he reported: "I tried it, and it works. After two weeks, I wasn't mad at that other guy any more. But you failed to make another important point, that this principle has a snowball effect. The next time I became angry with someone," he continued, "I prayed, and it didn't take two weeks to resolve the anger. The time after that it was even quicker. It's easy to feel differently about people if you're willing to pray for them."

There is the formula for beginning to develop a new, awake, alive congregation. Develop a method by which church people begin praying for one another.

A Methodist congregation in South Korea has 60,000 members with an average weekly Sunday school attendance of 25,000 (worship figures are considerably larger than that). The pastor attests that the secret of their phenomenal success is prayer. In the church building are 21 separate rooms used for nothing but prayer. A new prayer retreat has just been opened. Every morning at 5 a.m. more than 500 church members gather to begin the day with corporate prayer. When asked why daily prayer meetings were set at so early an hour, the pastor replied: "Because there are no conflicts. No one can say he has another something else to do at 5 a.m.!" The church is exploding with growth, and it all started (and is maintained) with prayer.

Numerous growing churches have established prayer groups as part of their regular church administrative team. The members are selected and asked to serve 12- to 24-month terms, just as others are selected to be trustees or members of the finance committee. The prayer group members meet every Sunday before worship and pray for the preacher, choir, all worship participants and for every person who comes through the church doors with some hidden need. Church rolls are divided alphabetically with names assigned to group members on a rotating basis, so that every week every member of the congregation is being prayed for by name. Every week someone is praying for Bob Allen: his health, his work, his family life and his soul. Someone else is praying for Susan Bishop and Fred Fox and Sherry Dunn — all the way down to the Zs. There is something about a program like that which pumps life and Spirit into a congregation. There is power in knowing (as a member of a church): "I matter to someone. Somebody is praying for me!"

A second indispensable for church growth and revitalization is The Bible. We are a people of the Word. Wherever and whenever that truth slips out of focus, our churches simultaneously slip out of gear.

John Wesley wrote in 1730: "I began to be 'homo unius libri' (a man of one book). I began to study (comparatively) no book but the Bible." In his preface to *Sermons On Several Occasions* (1746), he proclaimed again his intention to be "a man of just one book." This, of course, does not mean Wesley decided to become illiterate or uninformed where other writings were concerned. His personal records indicate that he had read from at least 1,400 different authors (with nearly 3,000 separate titles among them). What it did mean (as Albert Outler put it) was that "Wesley lived in the Scriptures and his mind ranged over the Bible's length and breadth and depth like a radar tuned into the pertinent data on every point he cared to make." Or, as Evelyn Laycock and James Holsinger state: "The Bible was his first and final norm for the validation of any theological discussion. His religion was a religion of the Bible."[4]

Those who have read Leader Keck's wonderful book *The Bible In The Pulpit* or have heard Fred Cradock lecture about remaining in The Word understand the intent of this thesis. Christians genuinely are (or should be) a people of The Book. Statistics consistently indicate that near the top of most visitors' checklists is not: "What will this church teach me about current issues or popular psychology or church history?" but rather, "Will this church share with me the truths of scripture?" Growing churches positively address that question from the pulpit, in the Sunday school classroom, in mid-week study groups, in cottage prayer meetings, in Disciples or Trinity Bible study courses. Growing churches place a high priority on teaching the Bible. As Elton Trueblood used to say, "We cannot have fruits without roots!"[5] The Christian's roots have always been securely fastened to the Word.

Ecumenical Bible study groups are sources of rich life and spirit within a local church. Often invitations extended to individuals at work or in the neighborhood to join such a group that meets one night per week renders unexpected and exciting dividends. Varied personal and theological perspectives are brought to a group when its membership is not limited to members of one congregation. Also, it is proven that persons who do not attend worship and are not officially affiliated with any particular local church are frequently interested in joining a group simply to study scripture. After a sufficient period of time meeting with a small group in such study, the church building itself begins to feel like home. Many a person who has agreed to attend a Thursday night informal Bible study in "your church" simply as a seeker of truth, given enough time, begins to think of the place as "my church." Frequently those persons go on to become committed and active members of the congregation, already having been effectively assimilated even prior to joining.

Prayer and The Bible: If we are serious about those things, our churches will feel "the wind of the Spirit" breathing life into the dry bones!

Another matter that is of singular importance is developing a good, solid small group structure in the local church.

Lyle Schaller has told us for years that within every congregation there are mini-churches (circles within the circle), and the people who stick with a church are the ones who find their needs being met in the smaller circle.

In the sanctuary one is part of a "congregation." In the Sunday school class, choir, youth group, men's or women's fellowship or a small Bible study class, for example, one becomes part of a "fellowship." In the larger circle one is relatively anonymous. In the smaller circle, somebody knows your name. One of the best means of evangelism at our disposal is the development and use of small groups that draw people into the fellowship.

In addition to such things as the Bible study groups already mentioned, other well-organized programs that address human

23

needs and personal interests are excellent avenues for persons to follow into a church. Many families eventually join a church because a son or daughter had become positively involved with a scouting program. Preschool (or Mom's Day Out) programs bring young families into contact with the church and help them learn to feel "at home" with a particular congregation. Sometimes it's an adult softball team that is the port of entry. Specific music programs for youth or children, special classes or other opportunities for persons with handicapping conditions, singles or single again groups or Parents Without Partners all become means of belonging to a small circle that is embraced by and part of the larger circle. Few things make people feel so warmly received as having a small group where someone knows their name, where they share a common interest and where they feel that they belong and matter. Those groups, if intelligently planned, become wonderful instruments of evangelism and church growth.

Intelligent planning is, of course, the key. It is never wise to answer questions people are not asking nor to offer food for which they are not hungry. About 20 miles outside a bustling southern city was a small, rural, white frame church with a new pastor fresh out of seminary. He was enthusiastic, if not altogether realistic. In short order, dreaming loftily, he convinced his church members that the city 20 miles away was growing in their direction and they should aggressively meet it. He convinced them of the urgent need to evangelize America's business and corporate community (a point at which he is no doubt correct). In any event, this young pastor talked his members into sponsoring a "Saturday Morning CEO Breakfast." Letters were sent out to 100 leaders in the business community. The letters explained the breakfast program and invited the execs to become participants. The women's group prepared breakfast on Saturday morning for 100 hungry businessmen. Saturday came, but they didn't. Not a single one of them showed up. Why not? Because leading CEOs in a large city are are not going to drive 20 miles out in the country to a little white frame church to eat pancakes and be preached to. The program was self-defeating from the very outset. However, another small church down the road heard about the idea and developed a reasonable variation. They sent letters and made phone calls to all the farmers in the area (hog farmers, dairy farmers, horse breeders, whomever). They offered a 6:30 a.m. breakfast on Thursdays with a brief program prepared by a representative of the county's Agricultural Extension Department. On the inaugural Thursday, 14 men attended. Now they have in excess of 20 per week (several of whom have become members of their church).

Small groups, intelligently planned, which address needs that people actually experience can become inexpressibly valuable tools not simply for offering authentic ministry to the community but also for building the spirit and size of a local congregation.

Mechanically, there is more or less a "Trinity" of indispensable foundations on which any local church can successfully build. Those foundations are prayer, The Bible and wisely planned small groups where people can nurture one another, where they can bond and be known.

Making It Work
In The Local Church

The local church remains the single most important institution in the world. It may have lost some of its luster over the past 20-to-30 years, but it is still irreplaceable. In fact, the future of our world and nation depends more on the church than on anything else at all.

The grass roots population understands the vital significance of the institutional church. Seventy-five percent of unchurched American adults still want their children to be actively involved in church.[1] Fifty-eight percent of those same unchurched adults readily confess that personal involvement in a local congregation would decidedly enhance their personal lives and are open to such if made to feel welcome and wanted.

In short, the church is still of paramount concern to people — even people who are functionally inactive with it. The task of the church is therefore to reclaim the spirit, power and influence that it can and should have within society at large. Any local church can do that if it remembers why it is in business.

Will Willimon and the late Dr. Robert Wilson say in *Re kindling The Flame* that "Each congregation needs to ask itself the questions: 'Who are we?' and 'What are we trying to accomplish?' "[2] That is a logical starting place for the local church that is interested in growth. It is imperative to understand what God has created and called us to do — why we are in business.

In *Megatrends*, John Naismith writes of the demise of railroads in America. He indicates the decline began to occur when railroad executives decided they were in the business of operating railroads. They forgot that they were actually in the business of transporting people. Richard Wilke has called that to our attention and likens the church to railroads. "Too many of us have come to believe that we are in the business of running the church; we are in the business of saving the

27

world!"[3] Ernest Fitzgerald tells the story of a beautiful gothic stone church in New York City which finally closed its doors. The lovely stained glass windows were boarded over. The once carefully manicured lawn was knee high. The massive oak doors were chained. On the front lawn, said Bishop Fitzgerald, was a "For Sale" sign. Beside it someone had placed a hand-painted cardboard sign with boldly printed words: "Our church went out of business because it forgot what its business was!"

As the church growth experts keep reminding us, local church revitalization begins when we remember what business we are in. According to Wilke, that is the business of saving the world. Evangelism is the heartbeat of that business. "Increasing numbers of people long for meaning in life, meaning not of their sole creation, meaning that gives their lives significance by joining them to some project greater than themselves."[4] Where can people be more effectively connected with that sort of meaning than in the church (if a church actually remembers and practices why it is in business)?

For purpose of review, let us re-state at this point that the church is still vital to the masses in our world. People do hunger and thirst for what it alone can offer. And if a church remembers why it is in business and practices that faithfully, people will still seek it out (often in rather impressive numbers).

Certainly the responsibility of making it happen in the local church is bi-focal. Both the corporate congregation and the ordained clergy have specific roles to play, and one without the other is (in Ben Franklin's words) "like half a pair of scissors."

Pollsters who do ecclesiastical studies indicate that church people basically desire two fundamental things of their ministers. In all honesty, clergy who are faithful to their calling owe their church people at least this much. The people in the pews desire (1) meaningful preaching and (2) attentive pastoring.

For ministers who would like to serve a growing church, here's how: preach with passion and pastor with compassion.

When that formula is followed with discipline and determination, local churches almost inevitably grow.

Preaching

Joe Harding, one of Protestantism's foremost voices in church growth and revitalization, contends that there is "unanimous agreement that without effective preaching, no matter how promising the situation or church location, renewal simply will not happen."[5] So far as breathing new life into the dry bones of a local church is concerned, there is no substitute for effective preaching.

Strong preaching, of course, requires work. Vital pulpits are rarely occupied by people who get started preparing the sermon on Saturday afternoon. Such practice insults not only the people ministers are called to serve but also the God who extended the call. There is no way to preach effectively without preparing effectively. Somewhere along the line, every minister makes his choices. If the choice is to busy one's self with 1,000 other issues instead of preaching, then the minister casts his lot with all the others who in Leander Keck's words "let sundry matters crowd out Sunday matters."[6] When that happens, worshipers will soon begin looking elsewhere come Sunday. Jesus' words to Martha are pertinent to too many clergy: "You are anxious about many things," but sometimes "only one thing is needful (Luke 10:14)."

John Killinger, the creative and knowledgeable homiletician, has written: "We become caught up in administrative duties, committee responsibilities, an endless road of telephone calls and letter writing, and the inevitable trivia of day-to-day existence, and before we know it these . . . lie squarely in the midst of our consciousness."[7]

The following poem was written about the structure of one of our leading denominations, but it could doubtless provide an adequate description of most denominations and our propensity for meetings:

29

Mary had a little lamb.
It could have been a sheep
Until it joined the _____ *Church*
And died from lack of sleep.

Fill in the blank with the name of your own part of the household of faith, and it is a fair guess that the poem will lose none of its originally intended accuracy. Growing churches have preachers who refuse to get caught in that trap, pastors who know how to prioritize and who faithfully carve out sacred time to prepare for preaching. Should they have to let something else go, so be it! The average church member will be enthusiastically supportive. They will readily forgive the minister's absence at a board of trustees meeting if they know it will mean a better sermon come Sunday morning.

Preparation time varies from minister to minister, but Buttrick's old thesis of an hour's preparation for every minute in the pulpit is still a rather reasonable formula to follow. Powerful preaching doesn't just happen. It takes labor . . . and time.

Though styles and methods differ, the following work routine for preaching provides solid results.

A — Themes should be plotted seasonally. It is helpful if the preacher knows his thematic destination no less than six months in advance.

B — When one knows where he is going, envelopes can be prepared for each upcoming sermonic theme. Appropriate illustrations, biblical references, observations, etc., can be placed in the envelope. Thus, when the week arrives for preparing that particular sermon, there will already be considerable fodder for the mill at one's disposal.

C — Monday is an ideal day for prayer and scripture study. During this time no real note-making is necessary (though some will inevitably take place). The purpose is simply to immerse one's self in the Spirit and the theme from a biblical perspective. If one is preaching from a Bible story, live with the story on Monday. Stay back in that time, listening to the voices of generations past. Move mentally into Jerusalem or Damascus, and do not hurry out. There is plenty of time for bridging the gap between the centuries as the week passes. Let The Word penetrate. Only in so doing will the preacher be familiar enough with "The" Word to make it "our" word.

D — Tuesday is the day to pick up one's pen and go to work. Most ministers find it advantageous to develop an outline. Outlines are like road maps. It is difficult to arrive at the proper destination unless a person knows where he is going. Ordinarily the Bible will provide all the outline the minister needs, if he has spent sufficient time with it. No one has to create an outline when preaching on the prodigal son (Luke 15). Luke gives us all the outline anyone could ever need:

1 — He rebelled;
2 — He repented;
3 — He returned;
4 — He was received.

Or take, for example, the parable of the neighbor at midnight (Luke 11:5-13):

1 — Cries for assistance;
2 — The hesitant helpfulness of humans;
3 — The tender helpfulness of a heavenly Parent.

The Transfiguration followed by the healing of the epileptic child is its own outline (Matthew 17:1-21):

1 — Fueled on the mountaintop;
2 — Sent to the valley.

Paul's pastoral letters are similar. So far as sermon preparation is concerned, Monday's journey into The Word ordinarily gives the minister a head start when it comes time to develop a solid outline on Tuesday.

E — Wednesday, Thursday and Friday mornings are spent writing, talking aloud, listening, re-writing and typing. The minister must grapple with a list of questions during the process:

"Am I moving from a written to an oral style?"

"Am I remaining true to the text?" (Always exegesis, never isogesis!)

"Is it thoroughly biblical?" Church growth experts know that people come to worship to hear the Bible's commentary on life, not the latest word from the fields of pop psychology or politics. They will go elsewhere for those commentaries. Lyle Schaller lists biblical preaching as the most important of all the characteristics he has discovered in growing churches.[8] Of course, "merely quoting the Bible is no guarantee of doing biblical preaching."[9] A text or biblical lesson should be employed, explored and applied helpfully to the world of the hearer. To blast the listener with verse after verse in shotgun fashion really accomplishes no significant end and, though sounding biblical, in the best sense really is not.

"Is my language accessible to all hearers, or am I too scholastic or too heavily theological?" Remember, we serve no noble purpose by preaching over anyone's head. To do so insults the listener and reflects poor preparation or excessive ego on the part of the preacher. This is why the sermon should be practiced aloud following the writing of the initial rough draft. As the preacher talks through the manuscript, he hears the places where editing should be done to make the sermon accessible (and to move it from the written to oral style).

"Am I letting the text speak or am I venting my own personal agenda items?"

"Is there good news in this sermon?"

"Is it properly illustrated?" The best way to bridge the gap between the centuries is to employ vivid, contemporary illustrations that place the biblical lesson within the framework of the listeners' world and experiences. Humor, references to theater, music or cinema, personal anecdotes in which the minister reveals himself as a fellow believer/pilgrim — all these forms of illustration make sermons more listenable and dramatically enhance their impact upon those who worship. Proper illustrating, of course, requires hard work. Illustrations must be carefully selected that are consistent with the theological integrity of the text. Good preachers don't just find an interesting story and "fit it in." If a story does not fit, it is not used. A time will come later when it is appropriate. Wait for that time. Meanwhile, dig harder and farther to find the right story, the one peculiarly suited for this particular pericope and for this particular moment in the flow of the message.

F — By Friday noon, the sermon should be in whatever form one will carry into the pulpit (manuscript, full notes, brief outline). At that poing it is wise to put the sermon away and rest the mind a bit by doing other things.

G — Most families seek uninterrupted time together on Saturday evenings. Preachers are better advised to schedule that time on Fridays. On Saturdays it is always helpful to cloister one's self to learn the sermon. This is done best by reading it aloud, pencilling in corrections that enhance an oral style. Then the minister should continue to preach the message aloud until he is able to do so comfortably, start to finish, without consulting the manuscript or notes. It is hard work, but it pays off on Sunday mornings by offering to the gathered listeners a well-prepared sermon that sounds spontaneous. Few things are less engaging than to have a manuscript read to an audience. Few things are more engaging than a well-prepared preacher who seems to be talking from the heart, empowered by the Spirit alone. To take a text, reach into someone's heart and touch that person with the Word for their world takes time, time, time and work, work, work.

Of course, even the most industrious preacher still runs the risk of answering questions that people do not ask, and thus failing to tap into this greatest resource for church growth and revitalization. Considerable attention should be paid to addressing themes that people are hungry to hear addressed.

What seems to work best in preaching for church growth is pastoral homiletics — in other words, concentrating on messages that address personal needs.

Listen to the voices:

From Will Willimon and Robert Wilson: "If you preach sermons that really relate to people's lives . . . (you) will bring the new members in."[10]

From John Killinger: "Real preaching grows out of the counseling session, the board meeting, the parish call, the casual encounter in a restaurant or grocery store. It speaks of and to what the minister has learned in all of his dealings with people during the week. It relates the gospel to human situations and works back and forth between them like a weaver's shuttle . . . . The preacher who is really serious about his or her calling should resolve early on never to preach a sermon that does not have the clear and statable aim of doing something for people!"[11]

From Phillips Brooks: "The preacher needs (always) to be a pastor!"[12]

From Evelyn Laycock and James Holsinger: "People whose lives are in disarray, whose souls need refreshing, whose thoughts flee to other times and places, whose spirits are despondent, all come to church at the worship hour in expectation. They expect that something transcendent may take place in their hearts and souls. They come hoping for a vital worship experience, a moment in which they meet a living God who can fill their inner emptiness with the fullness of purpose, hope and love."[13]

From Edgar Jackson: In *How To Preach To People's Needs* he wrote of a poll taken among church-goers. Of the nearly 4,000 who were interviewed, half felt that the major problems in their lives surfaced in such areas as futility, loneliness (75 percent of American adults will confess to experiencing loneliness at any given moment in time[14]), insecurity, inferiority, illness, sex, alcoholism, marriage and guilt. Approximately one-fourth were concerned with child training, separation, divorce, relational difficulties in the home, and other marital or domestic problems. Jackson estimated further that in any particular congregation, 20 percent of the people attending are dealing with grief, 33 percent of the married persons are unhappy at home, 50 percent are experiencing personal adjustment problems that threaten their security at school, work or in the community, 25 percent are depressed and 20 percent are so burdened with guilt or the fear of discovery that their peace of mind is seriously jeopardized. "There," he wrote, "are the people who come to our churches on Sundays seeking hope."[15]

In a meeting in Pawling, New York, in the autumn of 1989, Mrs. Ruth Peale was asked what, in her opinion, accounted for the enormous popularity of her husband, Norman's, preaching. Mrs. Peale never hesitated but offered the immediate reply: "That's easy. Norman's sermons touched lives because he steeped himself in the problems and pains of people."[16]

There is, without question, a noble place for prophetic preaching. But if church growth and revitalization is the topic, nothing has the impact of pastoral sermons — sermons that touch the hurts of broken-hearted people who occupy our pews Sunday by Sunday.

John Sutherland Bonnell, addressing a convocation of preachers, told of the Sunday when, at the close of worship at Fifth Avenue Presbyterian in New York City, he was greeting people at the back door. One woman (a visitor) lingered. When all others had left, she introduced herself to Dr. Bonnell. "You don't remember me, I'm sure," she began, "but I visited here two years ago. My daughter (who was eight then) had a tumor behind her left eye. We brought her to New York to an opthalmologist. To remove the tumor, he had to remove her eye. Now there is a tumor behind her right eye. Tomorrow they will remove it. This is the last day she will ever look at me — or at anything, for that matter." Then the mother began to cry. After composing herself somewhat, she continued: "I just came here today hoping to find the strength to face tomorrow." Then she walked away. Dr. Bonnell said that he watched her leave and thought to himself: "What in God's name . . . literally, what in God's name did I say today that can help that broken woman face tomorrow?"[17]

Without fail, every Sunday someone in the congregation is living on the edge of despair, hungering for some word that can help in facing tomorrow. Perhaps the leading church growth experts are correct in their virtually unanimous assessment that worshipers do not long for (nor are preachers ordinarily equipped to offer) the latest word on the political or social scene. Karl Barth put it this way: "We cut a ridiculous figure as village sages — or city sages. As such we are socially superfluous."[18]

Let us not misunderstand the point of all this: To ignore the social gospel is to ignore the gospel. The prophetic word is still required of preachers. Leonard Sweet observes that "authentic proclamation can never be personal at the expense of being prophetic." Dr. Sweet went on to say, however: "In like fashion, authentic proclamation can never be prophetic at the expense of being personal."[19] Many preachers who have laudatory track records in church growth and revitalization make it a practice that every sermon will have a primary pastoral thrust to it. Prophetic or social statements are not infrequent but always remain simply one point among several. Should the pastor be preaching one of those "milk-stool sermons" (the sort that always has three legs to it), he will often make the first point a social, missional or political statement. That will be followed by two other points that are uniquely personal and deal with such themes as God's grace and presence with us in our hours of need. Obviously, there is considerable thematic overlapping (e.g., the anxieties created by the Persian Gulf War of 1991 provided entree into the social and pastoral arenas with hardly a noticeable thematic transition).

Every Sunday people come to church bearing heavy crosses. Week by week they come with the question in their minds and hearts: "Does God have a word for me?" If that word is faithfully and regularly offered, those people will keep coming back, and they will bring others with them.

There is one other word of significance before the topic of preaching is concluded: Let it be biblical!

"Within Protestantism vital biblical preaching is the most important characteristic of growing churches."[20] Again to quote John Killinger: "Talking about God is more important than anything else we can do . . . How frustrated people are when the preacher talks about world issues without any reference to biblical theology, or discusses some psychological disorder without grounding it in the biblical understanding of persons, or delivers a lecture on marriage or education or the human predicament without tracing its roots in the community's dealings with God." He continues: "The greatest preachers have always been lovers of the Bible . . . The minister who would preach must come to love (the Bible), must live within its pages day by day, year by year, until it fairly saturates his or her being. He should pour over it the way people review old family albums, looking for their roots of existence in the faces and environments of days gone by, and reading the present and the future in light of the past."[21]

The Bible is our source of authority in the pulpit. Without it, preachers simply come off as the silly "village sages" Barth described.

If we wish to address prejudice, we can say: "Listen folks, this is what I think," and every hearing aid in the sanctuary will be turned off before we get to the second sentence. Is it not far better simply to let God's Word confront the people? "And Nathanael asked, 'Can anything good come out of Nazareth?' (John 1:46)." "And Peter said, 'Lord forbid that I should eat anything unclean.' (Acts 10:14)." "And the Pharisee prayed, 'Thank God that I am not like other men!' (Luke 18:11)."

If we wish to talk about forgiveness, we can say: "I know how you people live. You have no right to judge others or hold grudges. We must learn to get along in this world." Soon the snores will begin. It seems more effective simply to remind one's hearers: "You shall forgive your neighbor not seven times but seventy times seven (Matthew 18:22)." "And when you pray, say . . . forgive us our sins as we forgive those who sin against us (Matthew 6:12)." "Father, forgive them, for they know not what they do (Luke 22:34)." "This is my commandment, that you love one another even as I have loved you (John 15:12)."

If the topic is grace, what could be more effective than simply to say: "Now a certain father had two sons . . . And when he saw the younger son yet at a distance, he ran to him, embraced him, kissed him, put a ring on his finger and shoes on his feet and said: 'Kill the fatted calf! Let's have a party! For this, my child, was dead and is alive again. He was lost and is found!' " And the father's gate was never locked against his prodigal child (Luke 15:11-32).

If we choose to address the theme of compassion, how appropriate it is to say: "A certain man was journeying from Jerusalem to Jericho when he fell among thieves who stripped him and beat him and left him for dead . . . And there passed that way a Samaritan who went to him and bound up his wounds . . . Now I say unto thee, 'Go thou and do likewise!' (Luke 10:25-37)."

Authority for preaching is rooted squarely in the Bible. Scripture is far, far more than a mere jumping off place so one can get on with the stories and jokes. It is instead the foundation out of which all illustrations flow so that our age is bridged to the Bible's age and God's Word becomes a personal letter mailed to us.

Pastoral Care

Of similar importance is the second issue: pastoral care.

Laycock and Holsinger write: "A pastor to whom the people can relate in an intimate fashion is far more important than any other factor."[22] "Laypeople want pastors who are readily available when they are needed."[23]

All have heard horror stories of persons in intensive care units who waited for days for the pastor to arrive, only to be disappointed. Most have known persons who carried heavy burdens to ministers and received virtually no ministry. I personally recall a conversation with a friend who had been through the trials of cancer surgery. The attendant fears and anxieties were beyond measure. Before entering the hospital, he shared those fears and anxieties with his pastor and asked for special prayer and support. The minister told him quite frankly: "I will certainly keep you in my prayers. But, I really don't have the time to do visitation in the hospitals." Is it difficult to imagine why the patient went through a season of rather serious disenchantment with his church?

People in every parish are hurting. Forty-six percent of marriages fail. Countless others "stay together" but without thriving or any real mutual satisfaction. Parents tremble help-lessly at the knowledge their children are experimenting with drugs. Children likewise tremble in fear of alcoholic or abu-sive parents. The economy struggles, and persons who have not missed a day's work in 20 years are suddenly pounding the pavement seeking jobs. AIDS, cancer, cardiovascular dis-ease, diabetes. The very words strike fear in even the stoutest of human hearts. People need to know there is someone ac-cessible, someone who cares, someone who (whether or not he has the answers) hurts with them. Most turn first to their pastor.

Quite some time ago a member of the church where I pastor was hit by an automobile while crossing a city street. She went through long months of surgery, therapy and intense pain. On each occasion that our associate pastor or I visited with her, she would request that we hold her hand as we stood or sat at her bedside. During one of those visits the lady explained: "The touch of your hand keeps me from feeling so alone in my pain."

Church people need (and deserve) to know that they have ministers who are with them in their pain.

What, though, about corporate responsibility for making it work in the local church? Put another way: If the laity has the right to expect specific things of their pastors, what do clergy have the right to expect of their members? Consider five responses to that question.

1 — Church members are responsible to create a function-ing vehicle for "dreaming dreams and seeing visions (Joel 2:28)."

Most Protestant denominations have programs in place to assist local churches in this process (e.g. United Methodism's "Growth PLUS" or "Vision 2000" programs). Some vehicle is needed to help a church determine (a) where it wants to go and (b) where it can go in ministry as we prepare for the ar-rival of a new century.

Paula D'Arcy (quoted earlier) suggests that any church is wise to select a "think tank" committee that exists simply to listen to the Spirit's lead and project local church plans appropriately. That committee, she continues, should periodically conduct a "what if" exercise. It gathers and asks: "What if there were no church on this property? What if we were not a committee of an established church but rather a group of people planning to organize a new congregation? If that were the case, what do we think God would want a new church to do and be in this place during this time in history?" It is her contention (and a sound one) that when a committee answers those questions, it will know what God expects of its church, even if that church has stood on the same corner for the past 200 years.[24]

The membership of such a committee or task force (to be effective) should be chosen by the ministry staff. Any established nominations committee will continue to select "the old guard" or "favorite friends." A local church think tank group should instead be comprised of visionaries, newer members alongside members of long-standing who are not bound by the past. All should be committed to Christ and the local church. All should be responsibly evangelical. Recycling the same long range planning committee that has existed for 30 years will not suffice. Had they been pro-active, there would be no current need for such a committee to be considered. If this is to be a successful endeavor, let the make-up of the organization be new and fresh.

At an early meeting (perhaps the first following the organizational one), the following lists should be considered (with editorials appropriate to your local situation).

The "I Wish" List For The Local Church

The following questions must be addressed in visionary fashion. Thus, do not be concerned about our congregation's current ability or inability to finance your wishes. Dream big! Please feel free to use the back of the page to elaborate.

1 — I wish our facility could include:

2 — I wish the following position(s) could be added to our present staff:

3 — I wish there were support groups meeting regularly that addressed the needs of:

4 — I wish our church were more intentional in ministry to:

5 — I wish our church conducted worship services at times other than Sunday morning.   Y _____   N _____
If "Yes," what day? _____ time? _____

6 — I wish we identified prospective members in the following fashion(s):

7 — I wish we assimilated/nurtured new members in the following fashion(s):

8 — I wish our program of Christian education were more

9 — I wish our program of Christian education were less

10 — I wish our music program

11 — I wish our service(s) of worship

12 — I wish when people in our community heard the name of our church, they immediately thought of

13 — I wish our church's leadership circle were

14 — I wish God could get this one message through clearly to our church

15 — I wish we could get the message about our church out to a larger segment of the community, and think the best way(s) to accomplish that would be

Once the "I Wish" lists have been compiled, the pastoral leadership and members of the think tank organization can assess results. It is a good idea to distribute the survey in two or three phases (first, to the small leadership team that will ultimately assess results; second, to a larger group such as the church's official administrative body; and third, to the church at large). The leadership team needs to gather the survey forms and begin looking for trends. Those that emerge can then be placed under the egis of appropriate program teams or chairpersons to be pursued as part of the church's local ministry. The point is that church members are responsible to "dream dreams and see visions," and a creative pastor will locate (a) groups of pro-active thinkers and (b) useful format utensils to enable the task.

2 — Laity have a responsiblity for taking the lead in the ministry of identifying and visiting prospective members.

Herb Miller suggests that the average American adult will drive up to 15 minutes to attend church. Anything past that length of time becomes uncomfortable. That is amazing (since anything up to four hours for an athletic event is considered reasonable), but true. In any event, given Miller's observation, local church evangelism committees are well advised to find a large city map and draw a circle around the church, 15 minutes driving time in all directions. Whatever area appears inside the circle is the prime target area for evangelistic visitation. The questions then become: "Who lives inside the circle, and what does our church have to offer them?"

Initially local church personnel may have difficulty determining what socio-economic groups are most densely represented. Any local city planner's office can supply reams of demographical data that will prove helpful. Certain questions should be aggressively pursued:

a — Are there any baby boomers inside the circle? Baby boomers are those 77 million Americans born between 1946 and 1961. For a long time they have been conspicuously absent from mainline churches. But now, as a recent magazine article put it, "The Boomers Are Back."

"At one time or another, roughly two-thirds of the baby boomers dropped out of organized religion. But in recent years, more than one-third of the dropouts have returned. About 57 percent (43 million people) now attend church or synagogue. More than 80 percent of the boomers consider themselves religious and believe in life after death."[25]

Are they out there, within the circle? If so, what do those people need . . . and seek? There are a few clear and simple answers to that question. They seek relationship. They are weary with going it alone, one night stands and singles bars. Their youthful independent spirits are aging into ones that seek connection and relatedness. Many have decided that church is a good place to find the sort of "other" that can positively fill the inner emptiness they have too long been afraid to confess. They seek meaning which has not been secured in an abundance of things. As Patti Page voiced in song several years ago, baby boomers have acquired and attained only to ask: "Is That All There Is?" They seek direction from beyond (i.e., a sense that this is a friendly universe and that they are not aimlessly wandering through a pointless maze). Life, to be full, has to be possessed of purpose. Those who are married (especially with children) seek a church setting that will enhance family life and values. They are more interested in clean nurseries, attractive children's wings and marriage enrichment retreats than in gothic sanctuaries and medieval baroque anthems. Church evangelism committees (if functioning properly) will determine if the baby boomer generation is represented inside the circle and what the church must do to offer them authentic ministry.

b — Are there singles represented inside the circle on the map? Many contend that singles and single-agains comprise the most fertile ground for church growth and evangelism of any group in the '90s. They certainly represent a sizeable segment of the adult population in America (with estimates ranging from 35 to almost 45 percent). By the turn of the century well over half the adult population will be single, and currently almost half of our nation's graduating high school seniors come from single parent homes. Thus, any church that ignores ministry to singles is effectively shutting the door on its major field of prospective members.

The simple truth is, any church can provide a singles ministry. It only takes a room to meet in, a steering committee and a willingness to do a bit of public relations. More than any other group at all, singles tend to take the reins and manage the program themselves once it is established. Statistics prove that churches which offer any special opportunities for singles (be it Sunday school or week night fellowship) tend to reap the benefits in terms of increased membership.

c — Are there senior adults in the circle? Too often persons assume that older adults have already made all the decisions they are going to make. Such is not necessarily the case, even as it has to do with religion and church affiliation.

One senior adult couple who live in a small Texas town had for years been inactive in church. He was an Episcopalian. She was a Roman Catholic. They compromised by staying home from both denominations. Today they are very active, rarely missing a Sunday at "their" church (which, by the way, is neither Episcopal nor Catholic). How did the change in worship habits occur? Very simply, a neighbor took the time to stop by and invite them to visit her church. That's all there was to it. Someone dared to believe that God is still able to do marvelous things with persons who preceded the baby boomers by several years. The couple in question told their new pastor that the woman who invited them was the first person in 14 years to ask them to visit in church."[26] Often a simple invitation is all that is required: a willingness to ask and a genuine interest in the one whom we are asking.

Senior adults offer a wide variety of strengths to local churches. They have more free time at hand than their counterparts who have not yet retired. With advances in health care and longer life expectancies, they are frequently the beneficiaries of strength and energy that some find surprising (even enviable). Obviously they possess more experience than those who have not yet lived so long. Time, energy and experience add up to the potential to become unusually productive members of the church family. Most are waiting simply to be asked.

d — Are there youth in the circle? Eighty percent of America's children are not in church on Sunday mornings. Seventy-five percent of our teenagers are involved in some fashion of sexual experience on Saturday nights. Roughly 40 percent get drunk or high as frequently as once per week. And alarmingly increasing numbers have so despaired of life that they are choosing suicide as an option to be pursued. On every hand there is evidence that children and youth, overwhelmed by and afraid of life, are checking out (some by physically or chemically anesthetizing themselves; others by pulling the trigger). Our young people need hope, and apparently for many it is hard to find. That's where the church comes in. We are stewards of hope. There is (as Elton Trueblood put it in the title of his book) an *Alternative To Futility*. The alternative is relationship — with Christ and with a community of people who love unconditionally, even as we are loved.

Youth choirs, inviting Sunday night youth fellowships that effectively balance biblical study with recreation and opportunities for sharing in an environment free of judgment, scouting programs, caring leaders who can serve as listeners and friends and even facilities that indicate a place for and commitment to youth go far in salvaging desperate young lives as well as nurturing other ones. Likewise, this investment of time, love and money brings certain returns for the local church. It is undeniable that active youth and children tend to reactivate parents and grandparents who have grown ecclesiastically lazy. Are there young people in the circle? What does the church offer (or plan to offer) them?

Other target groups can be listed, many unique to the particular local church implementing a program of prospective member visitation. The point is that no church can reap much of a harvest if it does not know what is growing in the field.

In some instances, for example, without doing our homework a church may go to great lengths to develop a ministry to singles when in fact it has a much higher density of senior adults living within minutes of its steeple. Examine the turf. Know the territory. Aggressively pursue the target groups. And be certain that once they attend, the church has in place some program of ministry tailored to their needs.

Obviously the laity carry the lion's share for doing the prospective member visitation. However diligent a pastor may be, he cannot do evangelistic visitation alone. In fact, laity do it far more effectively from a statistical standpoint. Most stats indicate that first time visitors who are contacted in person by lay church members tend to return in rather impressive numbers (roughly 80 percent if visited within 24 hours, 60 percent if visited within 48). Interestingly, if clergy make the initial visit, the return ratio is reduced by virtually 50 percent. Why is that? Very simply, that phenomenon exists because people expect clergy to visit. It is viewed as being their job. However, when a lay member of a congregation stops by to say "We were glad you visited in our church today," that is viewed as hospitality.

Let it be noted by all that visitation teams should visit! Telephoning prospective members is better than nothing but will never compare in results with the effectiveness of face-to-face contact. Cards and letters are even less productive. "Contact people in person — not through the mail. Paper never substitutes for the influence of personality!"[27]

Encourage the visitors (who, by the way, should go out in twos — husband and wife teams are usually effective, though by no means required) to be direct about who they are and why they have come. "Hi. We are Gerald and Iris Smith from Northport Church. We understand you visited with us this morning and would like to come in for just a moment to say, 'Welcome to Northport.' " It is genuinely important to enter the house. Screen doors that remain closed between resident and visitor represent barriers to relationship. Front porch evangelism rarely accomplishes much. George Morris suggests that

15 minutes in the living room is helpful and 15 in the den, even better. Five minutes at the kitchen table with a cup of coffee, and one can almost certainly remove that person's name from the prospect's list and inscribe it on the church roll. Getting in the house (if such can be done graciously and non-aggressively) is of paramount significance.

Beyond debate is the value of having the visitation team carry with them to each home some printed material about the church. Those items give the prospect time to peruse what the church has to offer at his leisure after the visit is completed. Likewise, a memento of interest is a winning idea. In other words, have the visitors carry something that says "Welcome. You are important to us." Some visitation teams carry pies or home-baked bread. Equally effective (and less fattening) are potted plants with a card naming the church and including a catchy phrase such as "Come grow with us!" Placed on a window sill, every time the person passes through the kitchen and sees the plant she will think of the church it represents.

Visitors should be encouraged never to overstay their welcome. Fifteen minutes is ordinarily the optimum length of stay (10 is better). Past that the encounter tends to become counter-productive (and even produces decreasing results). Visitors should leave at the pinnacle of the encounter, not when it is on a declining curve.

Once the in-home contact has been completed, church visitors should immediately fill out a prospective member information card. Such a card should be done in duplicate (one for the committee's files and one for the senior minister or minister of visitation). On page 49 is a sample of how a three-by-five index card should be used.

Follow-up visitors should examine notes on the cards prior to making contact. This will enable them to address pertinent issues and not simply to re-plow introductory ground. Also, this proves an invaluable resource to pastors who are also making contact with prospective members (providing insight into personal pastoral needs or skills and abilities that would be of service to church or community).

Front Side of Card

Name(s): _____ Visit made by _____

_____ Date: _____

_____ How long in town: _____

Date when prospect visited our church: _____

Address: _____ Phone No. _____

Marital/Family status: _____

Current church affiliation: _____

(Over)

Back Side of Card

Notes: Use this side of card to include brief personal data. E.g., why did they visit our church? Who brought or invited them? Are they actively involved in another local church? Are there children in the home? What ages? Any information regarding personal needs (What are they looking for in a church family)? Any relevant information about former church background or areas of service.

There will be occasions, of course, when evangelism team visitors can assist the ministers to make more effective use of their time by editing the visitation list. A noted mountain wood artist (we used to call them "whittlers" before the trade became sophisticated) was asked how he carved such life-like canine figures. He answered simply: "Well, ah jest take mah knife and mah block a' wood, and ah whittle away ever'thing that don't look like a dawg!" Evangelism team visitors serve a valuable purpose by "whittling away" first-time visitors who are not legitimate prospects for church membership. For example, a notation on the back of the three-by-five card may read as follows: "This couple was in church on Feb. 9 because their son's scout troop was recognized. Ordinarily they attend First _____ Church, where they are active members. No need to visit." The minister can then send a form letter/card welcoming the family to church and devote his attention to visiting in other homes where needs or potential are real.

Many churches find it effective to make evangelism team members visible on Sunday mornings. Marble Collegiate Church in New York City, for example, has their team members wear red carnations and stand at the altar at the close of the morning worship service. Visitors are encouraged to speak with team members to secure information about the church. Boone United Methodist (NC) stations its team members near all exits from the sanctuary. They, too, are identified by the use of carnations. Visitors naturally pass by their stations, whereupon they are given printed information (church profile booklets and recent newsletters) about the church. Ben Hill Church in Atlanta has visitors stand up during the service, and evangelism team members go to them in their pew with the outstretched hand of fellowship. In each of those cases (as with virtually all growing churches), the evangelism workers secure information about the first-time visitors so that follow-up can be made.

What About Evangelism Committee Meetings?

Q — How often should evangelism teams/committees meet?

A — Monthly

Q — What is a helpful format?

A — Begin with prayer. A brief devotional based upon a lesson that is essentially evangelical is also a plus. This is, after all, a spiritual endeavor that must have a strong spiritual base in order to be successful.

The meeting then turns to a review of contacts made by visitation teams over the past month. Current status of the prospects contacted is discussed (e.g., Are they still attending? Have they become involved in any church activity other than worship?) Based upon these reports, decisions are made regarding the advisability of visiting the person/family in question again during the following month. If they are to be re-visited, responsibility for making contact is passed along to a new visitation team.

Persons who have initiated contact with the church are considered next. This may include individuals/families who have visited in the church at worship, Sunday school or for other special events. It may also include persons newly involved in ongoing church activities (e.g., scouting, day care, senior adult fellowship, etc.). Assignments are made linking those persons to a visitation team which will make personal contact prior to the next meeting.

Third, the committee will consider any referrals from the pastoral staff or church members at-large. Once it is known that a person is involved in evangelism/church growth ministries, frequently he is stopped in the hall of the church (or business or grocery store) by someone who says: "If you ever get the chance, would you mind putting _____ on your list of folks to be visited? He works with me and isn't involved in church anywhere. I think he might be interested if someone reached out."

Finally, the committee will deal with its own personal circle of relationships. The FRAN Model[28] is a helpful and reasonable approach. "FRAN" is an acronym for friends, relatives, acquaintances, neighbors. It simply means that committee members will brainstorm about functionally unchurched persons in their own close circle of relationships. Those persons are strong candidates for membership in the church family. After all, they are already personally involved with active members. A trust level has been previously established. And probably (through contact and association) they have been appraised of what the church in question is like. The gardening has been done. It simply remains to reap the harvest. Assignments of visitors are made.

The evening should end as it began: with prayer. Prayer circles, hands held, are effective symbols of the business of the team (being one with Christ and one with each other, close bound in spirit and purpose). Many committee chairpersons use this closing prayer as a ceremony of commissioning (or sending forth).

A good rule of thumb: It should not take long periods of time to do lots of work. If properly organized, no committee meeting should require more than 90 minutes. Sixty is even better.

Q — Are there effective evangelism programs currently available to local churches?

A — Yes. Consult headquarters. Every denomination has a program. "Church Grow" (from the National Evangelistic Association in Lubbock, Texas) and "Vision 2000" or "Growth PLUS" (from the Board of Discipleship, The United Methodist Church) are examples that come to mind. All denominations have in-house local church evangelistic packages. With minor variations, most are strikingly similar. All are helpful to some degree. The committee should examine resources and decide upon a program that seems uniquely suited to the local situation. Of course, many may choose simply to use the prospective member identification/visitation/assessment/follow-up format listed previously in the question-and-answer segment of this chapter. If aggressively pursued, this format is almost certain to insure church growth.

Two Do's And One Don't

1 — Do practice observational evangelism. This simply means training the laity of the church to be aware of new persons in their circles of relationships who are functionally unchurched. It is fundamentally more a matter of mind-set than effort. A new family moves into a house down the block, a new person takes a position in the office, a child begins dating a youth new to his school. Inquiry is made regarding how long the person has been in the community. If the person/family is a new arrival and thus has not yet established a church home, word is passed along to the Evangelism Committee and contact is made. Many individuals find this sort of evangelistic commitment less threatening than going out and knocking on doors. It only requires keeping one's eyes and ears open and then passing along information to others who do not mind making personal contact.

2 — Do practice hospitality evangelism. Basically this is just a matter of making certain that first-time (or repeat) visitors to one's church are not lost in the shuffle. Greeters, ushers and the deployment of easily identifiable evangelism committee members at entrances and exits makes "hospitality evangelism" one of the church's simplest tasks. It requires nothing more strenuous than to offer gestures of warmth and welcome to strangers in our midst. (Note: Greeters should not wear badges that read "Greeter." That indicates to a visitor that the man/woman with the badge has been assigned a Sunday to be friendly. Far better is to wear lapel identification that

reads "Host" or "Hostess." Ken Kroehler of First United Methodist Church, Lancaster, Pennsylvania, has his greeters wear badges that ask" May I help you?" The object is to aim for warmth, inclusiveness and hospitality.)

Herb Miller writes: "People are looking for a place where they can find a warm relationship with other people. They are looking for people who care about each other and will give them an opportunity to become part of the group. Everyone wants to be wanted."[29] Provide visitors with the sense that here they are cared about, here they are wanted and here they can belong, and those visitors will become the beneficiaries of a fashion of Christian hospitality that generally will lead them to unite with the church.

Hospitality evangelism also obviously includes what many refer to as decision calls. Simply put, that means issuing invitations to attend church as well as to unite with it. Whereas the latter may traditionally be more the work of the clergy, the former is more effectively the work of the laity. Growing churches have lay members who are not timid about inviting persons to attend church. Should that not be the mind-set of a particular congregation, moving the church's personality from introversion to extroversion will require a systematic and determined approach on the part of minister and evangelism committee. Sermons, church school lessons, special studies and training sessions on invitational evangelism will need to be preached, taught and conducted. Be well assured that the return is more than worth the investment. As Joe Harding and Ralph Mohney have observed: "Churches that invite, grow. Churches that do not invite, decline."[30] It really is that simple . . . and that crucial.

3 — Don't confuse the evangelistic agenda with any reclamation project regarding inactive members.

One of the first comments frequently made when evangelism committees meet is: "I think before we go out looking for new members, we ought to do something to get back the members we already have who do not attend." As soon as that statement is made, the evangelism agenda is ordinarily

(a) diluted and/or (b) abandoned altogether. The reclamation of inactive members (an extraordinarily difficult task, since most members who left a church did so intentionally, with what they assessed to be a valid reason, and therefore are not likely to do an about-face) is not the business of the evangelism committee. It is the business of the membership care committee or the shepherding task force. Evangelism is to take the story to persons beyond the ecclesia and draw them in.

The Serious Business Of Worship

Though the urgency of preaching has already been addressed, it cannot be left unsaid that the overall experience of worship (including liturgy, sacrament and music) remains a vital issue in church growth. It is virtually undeniable that people look first to the impact of the worship experience in determining whether or not to return to a church for a second visit. And though the preached Word is the primarily determining factor in assessing worship, it is not by any means the only factor. In truth, many a strong sermon has been negatively compensated for by weak liturgy or music. Conversely, many a worshiper goes home feeling closer to God not because of the merit of the sermon but rather due to the strength of the service in which the sermon was merely one component.

Whether a particular congregation employs "high church" or "low church" liturgy does not ordinarily radically affect growth patterns. What does seem to be important is whether the worshipers are treated as audience or actors. An audience simply witnesses a performance by others. An actor participates in the drama. It is the latter approach that is regularly evident in growing churches.

Involvement of the worshiper in the ongoing drama of worship can be attained in numerous ways. Consider, for example, the following suggestions (realizing that within each congregation, numerous other suggestions unique to the local situation will surface):

a — Use of frequent corporate litanies (e.g., calls to worship, creeds and responsive readings).

b — Creative use of prayer time (prayers of bidding; corporate prayers of confession or thanks; use of The Lord's Prayer following the pastoral prayer; asking the worshipers to join hands during prayer time, including moments when each person is asked to pray silently for the others whose hands

57

he is holding; inviting worshipers who so desire to come forward and kneel at the altar as the morning prayer is offered; allotting time each Sunday for silent prayers and meditations).

c — Involvement of lay members of the congregation in the service of worship (offering the morning or offertory prayer; making the announcements or highlighting special announcements pertaining to that lay member's area of responsibility; being the lector and leading creeds or reading scripture lessons).

d — Create within the worship experience informal moments when persons feel free to offer brief spontaneous remarks (e.g., announcements from the floor, prayer requests).

e — Children's time within the worship service, where children are free and encouraged to enter into dialogue with the story leader; story leader can and should be a lay person with talents for and interests in children's ministries.

f — If persons with appropriate skills are members of the congregation, the use of liturgical drama or dance can also be meaningful and inclusive.

g — Baptismal liturgies should involve the entire worshiping congregation in the liturgy and celebration.

h — Seasonal observances such as Advent candle and Lenten cross devotionals can be led by lay members (either as singles or family units).

i — Feature children and youth as frequently as possible.

j — Offer coffee hours following worship, where individuals who were just part of the "congregation" can become part of the "fellowship."

The list of appropriate, workable ideas is almost without end. A creative pastor and worship committee can determine methods of increasing lay involvement in the worship experience that will protect and enhance worship rather than detract from it. Whenever that is done, worship attendance and church membership tend to increase (often dramatically).

A congregation's sacramental posture is likewise important. In truth, so far as church growth is concerned it matters little whether a church serves communion weekly or quarterly.

What does matter is the worshiper's perception of the relative importance of the sacrament vis-a-vis the rest of the worship agenda. Communion that seems "tacked on" is rarely a high impact event, even if the sacrament is observed each Sunday. On the other hand, a quarterly communion service that underscores the reverence, mystery and power of the occasion may draw worshipers into the very presence of God. The point is, quantity does not matter half so much as quality.

In an age where the validity of word and table has become almost universally affirmed, services that highlight sacrament (whether communion or baptism) should not exclude the preached Word. Indeed, scaled down models (sometimes referred to as mini-sermons or meditations) are almost as inadequate as no sermon at all. Even as sacrament provides a needed sense of the presence of Christ, so does sermon provide a needed sense of his word for the living of these days. Neither should be underemphasized. In growing churches, neither is.

Of particular importance is music. That is to a worship experience what a thermostat is to a room. It can warm the setting up or cast a deadly chill over it.

Ralph and Nell Mohney, who did a study of the fastest growing congregations of a leading Protestant denomination,[1] suggest that dying churches provide music for musicians while growing churches provide music for the masses. Certainly they are not implying that churches should sell their pipe organs and install moog synthesizers instead. Rather they are observing that musical tastes vary (and develop) from generation to generation, and living, vital churches are sensitive to that. It is unreasonable to think that youth and young adults who listen to pop, adult contemporary or country music all week will suddenly develop an appetite for Mendelssohn upon crossing the portals into a sanctuary. Even some of the hymns written by saints like Charles Wesley (hymns deemed in every setting tasteful and appropriate) were frequently popular pub tunes with words of faith substituted in place of their secular counterparts. In other words, the accepted hymn masters of the ages understood that tune and style are simply vehicles of the message. There is a significant difference between a church and a college of music. Churches that confuse those two entities tend to develop a musical arrogance that is insensitive to the worship needs of the majority of persons seeking ministry in that setting.

Some time ago columnist Lewis Grizzard wrote a tongue-in-cheek article about church music that probably resonated with the feelings of the vast majority of faithful church attenders in most of our major denominations. The old adage "many a truth is said in jest," has merit. Such was certainly the case so far as Grizzard's article was concerned. Consider this excerpt:

> *"There's one more reason why I think a lot of people — and I am certainly included — don't darken the doors of church as often as they once did.*
>
> *It's church music. Something has happened since I left . . . the church so dear to my childhood."*

Then Grizzard went on to name a few of his personal favorites, the hymns he sang growing up as the song leader led the congregation (a useless formality since everyone there knew all the old favorites by heart): "Precious Memories," "The Old Rugged Cross," "Just As I Am," "Love Lifted Me," "In The Garden," "Peace In The Valley," "Power In The Blood," "Nearer My God To Thee." He continued:

> *"They rarely sing any of those songs when I go to church nowadays . . . The last time I was married, I went to a Presbyterian church to which my wife belonged. Nice church. Nice people. Great minister. But I'd never heard of a single song they sang.*
>
> *I went to another Methodist church a few weeks ago. No Cokesbury hymnal, and a woman in the choir got up and sang what sounded like something from an opera and hurt my ears."[2] (Note: Grizzard in his column referred to two specific denominations. This author suspects that*

his remarks could just as easily be applied to many, if not most, local churches in all the major Protestant denominations throughout America.)

Of the hymns Grizzard listed as his personal favorites, competent musicians would rightly attest that there is not a single piece of high quality music included. His point is that those pieces are particularly familiar. For significant portions of a congregation they conjure up images of other days that were important in individual spiritual journeys. They carry people back to Beth' El in ways that are personally powerful and cannot be denied. Thus, the value of those familiar hymns cannot be underestimated. The purpose they serve in returning one to his spiritual roots is sacred. Let it be re-stated: There is a profound difference between a church and a college of music.

The use of contemporary Christian music, as well as the inclusion of familiar hymns, serves a valid purpose for churches that are interested in meeting the needs of all age-level constituencies. Few teenagers carry tapes of Wagner or Mozart in their jam boxes. However, they may be very at home with the style of Amy Grant or Sandi Patti.

A reasonable (and healthy) approach to the ministry of music is to make it inclusive. In other words, provide a varied menu. Churches such as the Crystal Cathedral in Garden Grove, California, have succeeded in making their music ministries attractive to virtually all who gather on Sunday mornings. Those who have attended services in that particular church (or watch via television) realize that it is not at all out of the ordinary in one Sunday's service for the chancel choir to do a classical anthem by Bach followed shortly by an appearance by Larnelle Harris singing his latest gospel rock recording. All musical tastes (and needs) are taken seriously and addressed within the same service.

Many growing churches find that traditional, classical anthems coupled with contemporary Christian offertories are, in fact, complementary and provide all who come with the message that their needs are taken seriously.

The bottom line is simply this: Church music is ministry, not performance. It is meant to praise God and to put people in touch with God. No more should classical music be expunged from the repertoire than should folk or contemporary Christian music be avoided. In growing churches, all styles are employed since all people of all tastes are important.

Worship remains at the heart of what the church is and does in the world. Persons seeking a church home will inevitably be primarily influenced by the quality of the worship experience. Liturgy, the inclusion of lay involvement in the service, sacrament and music (along with) the spoken Word) are the key factors that an individual will use in determining whether or not a worship experience ministered effectively to his spiritual needs. Churches that want to grow will not underestimate the critical nature of planning effectively and implementing carefully and thoughtfully all aspects of worship. It is that public moment when a church has a singular opportunity to put its best (or worst) foot forward to the community.

Christian Education

Too long the role of Christian education (and especially the Sunday school) in church growth has been underestimated. The truth is, the strength of the Sunday school is directly related to the plausibility of growth within virtually all local congregations.

Historically this precedent cannot be denied. Luther and Calvin were fundamentally Christian educators (whose works formed and fashioned the entire Protestant movement). John Wesley in 18th century England established within the Anglican Church an experience called "the class meeting." It consisted of lay persons gathering in homes, reading and discussing the Bible. That Bible study movement gave birth to Methodism. (Note: As previously indicated, Mr. Wesley referred to himself as "*homo unius libri* [a man of one book]," meaning that all his thoughts, words and actions would be fashioned and judged in light of scripture.) At Oxford he and his brother, Charles, joined with other like-minded Christian students in rising early and beginning each day with intense Bible study around 5 a.m. Wesley's conversion experience (in a chapel on Aldersgate Street in May of 1738) occurred as he listened to someone read from Luther's preface to the book of Romans and suddenly felt overcome by the message of grace contained in that work. The story is told and re-told as one looks at the life line of any given denomination. At its point of origin there is the profound and moving influence of Christian education, and church growth took place as a result of persons who were hungry to know God's truths and had their hungers fed.

The rapid and strong development of Protestantism on the North American continent was to a great extent due to the early contributions of persons like Horace Bushnell, a pioneer of Christian education. In short, throughout its history, where church growth has been evident, a strong, unshakable commitment to Christian education has been likewise evident.

For unknown reasons, over the past 25 years the church in America has become more activist and less educational. Reason dictates that the one cannot effectively exist without the other, but a strong effort was expended to disprove reason. The results were disastrous.

Evelyn Laycock, writing of one major denomination which simply illustrates what was ongoing in virtually all major Protestant denominations from the late '60s to the mid-'80s, observes: "Within the General Board of Discipleship, the percentage of funds . . . allotted to education decreased from 21 percent to 16 percent" from 1975 - 1986.[1] During that period of time, her denomination's membership decreased by almost a million persons. Pick a major Protestant denomination. Its story will have been remarkably similar.

Where the commitment to Christian education has remained significant, churches within denominations of declining membership have not similarly declined. Take, for example, the case of United Methodism (the largest Protestant denomination in the world). Over the course of 25 years, its membership in the U.S.A. has declined from more than 12 million to just under nine million. An interesting phenomenon has become evident regionally. Over those years, the decrease in membership in the southeastern jurisdiction of the nation has been less than four percent.[2] In many areas of the southeast (e.g., the episcopal areas of Florida, North and South Carolina and Virginia, among others), United Methodist membership is currently increasing. However, while the southeast lost less than four percent and many of its areas have begun to grow, nationwide the denomination's decline had been more than 22 percent. Is there a key factor that one could identify to explain the difference? Some would argue that population migration to the sun belt is an answer. Recent census figures, however, make that argument more dubious than many previously believed. Northern and mid-western industrial regions are not quite so near death as suspicions implied, and even in most areas of declining population there remains a 56 percent slice of the census pie that is functionally unchurched.

Instead, the key may lie in regionally-based philosophies of Christian education. In many areas of the northeast, it is the practice of local churches to provide Sunday school opportunities on the same schedule as public school (thus closing the Sunday school program for the months of June-August). That practice negatively affects virtually every other program of : : church (including worship attendance, stewardship and church growth). Obviously an individual or family moving into a new community and looking for a church home will be more attracted to a congregation with a 12-month program than a nine-month program.

Some Suggestions For Maintaining A Strong Program Of Christian Education That Is Attractive To Potential New Members

1 — Always operate Sunday school on a 12-month basis. To do less is to encourage prospective members to shop elsewhere for a church home.

2 — Develop one new adult Sunday school class at least every other year. Otherwise new/prospective members face the difficult task of trying to find acceptance in a club that has already bonded.

3 — Offer a reasonable variety of adult classes. Not everyone has the same needs/appetites for Christian education. There should be:

- Couples classes (for young, mid-life and senior adults).
- Singles and singles-again classes.
- Lecture style classes employing the International Lesson Series curriculum.
- Discussion classes employing a similar, biblically based curriculum.
- Topical classes which address issues of current concern from the perspective of faith.
- Ongoing membership training classes (preferably taught by someone on the staff). These should be no longer than

six weeks in duration and should deal with such themes as: denominational identity, local church program, what new members can expect of their relationship with this particular congregation, what this congregation expects of its new members, etc.

- At least one class that provides the opportunity for genuine integenerational fellowship.

4 — Publicize the importance of the Sunday school through:

- Announcements in the weekly bulletin;
- A regular "What's Happening in Sunday School" column in the church newsletter;
- Inviting teachers or class representatives to share brief, pertinent information about current class studies or projects during the congregational concerns segment of the morning worship service;
- Monthly Sunday school moments during worship, with pastor or Christian education director introducing a different teacher, class format and curriculum each month.

5 — Express appreciation! Everyone likes to know that his work is appreciated. Though praise is never the motivation behind authentic Christian service, jobs well done should not be taken for granted. "Thanks" may be a small word, but it is great in importance. Simple ideas that express appreciation and keep good teachers stimulated for further service include:

- Annual teacher installation ceremonies during worship on Promotion Sunday.
- Teacher Recognition Sunday during autumn or spring, when Sunday school teachers are identified with carnations and small gifts presented at the altar, and the theme of the service (including the sermon) deals with the valuable ministry of Christian education.
- Bi-annual hand-written "thank you" notes to all teachers and classroom workers from either the education chairperson or the pastor.

• An annual teachers' appreciation banquet at the church that blends recognition for jobs well done with a motivational address from an inspiring speaker (preferably someone not on the local church staff).

The local church's program of Christian education, of course, is not limited to what occurs on Sunday mornings. Growing churches recognize the importance of providing ongoing weekly study opportunities for adults and youth. Statistically speaking, growing churches offer frequent weekday Bible study classes. A plethora of strong curricula is available, from Disciples to the Trinity Bible plan to the Bethel Bible series virtually *ad infinitum*. Those programs have the potential of significantly increasing persons' understanding of the biblical story, which almost without fail subsequently deepens commitments to the church in which the story was learned.

One of the key benefits of ongoing small group Bible studies has to do with group dynamics. As previously noted in the section on "Prayer Power, Bible Power And Small Group Dynamics" (and likewise indicated regarding coffee hours following worship) small study groups transport a person from being part of the "congregation" to being part of the "fellowship." Ordinarily group members who spend one or two hours together weekly following a format of sharing, prayer and Bible study experience such significant bonding that they become spiritual "family" to one another. Few things strengthen commitments to a local church so much as the feeling that one is wanted and belongs. Such is the regular (and predictable) result of small weekday/night study groups. Warren Hartman notes in his book *Five Audiences* that the small group dynamic meets personal social and spiritual needs as nothing else can within a church, resulting not only in faith development but also in new commitments by group members to Christian discipleship.[3]

Obviously a key factor in either the Sunday school or the small group study unit is leadership. How does one go about selecting, securing commitments from and training potential leaders? The following check-list is helpful.

1 — Select persons who have demonstrated interest in biblical studies (and have evidenced such through participation in other study groups).

2 — Select persons who are reasonably at ease on their feet in front of groups. Few things distract from desired group dynamics so much as a leader who is obviously unsure of his leadership abilities and/or materials.

3 — Select persons who have no personal nor theological scores to settle. Everyone respects those who have principles to defend and placards to carry. However, that should be done in a setting other than an organized group endeavor of Christian education. In that setting, leaders are guides on a quest for truth and not standard-bearers of any one particular dogma.

4 — Select leaders who are personable, warm and winning. Even a firm command of the subject does not ordinarily offset a sour countenance or negative disposition.

5 — Assure teachers that they are not taking a position "till death do us part." Solicit commitments to teach by promising definite tenure (12 to 18 months). Then, honor the promise! It is good for both teacher and group (protecting the one against burn-out and the other against a narrowness that is inevitable when listening to only one perspective on subject material).

6 — Continuity of leadership is a key for newly formed and developing classes. Thus, it is better when possible to have one leader than a rotating leadership team. Children and adults need consistency in a classroom. To persons of all ages it seems that a familiar face at the board or lectern is reassuring. We learn more effectively when someone trusted appears to be "in control." Thus, prospective teachers should be asked to devote regular attention to classroom duties for the designated period of 12 to 18 months. It is reasonable to assure the prospective teacher that an assistant will be secured, allowing the primary teacher the privilege of one Sunday's freedom from responsibilities per month.

7 — Prospective teachers should be invited to join the pastor and/or Christian education director in selecting classroom

curriculum. It is never advisable to ask a person to teach material with which he is not fully comfortable.

8 — Training for new teachers can be done privately in consultation with the pastor and/or Christian education director. Or, a general training session for all teachers can be scheduled prior to Promotion Sunday. The latter would require various orientation personnel to train leaders along age level lines.

9 — The pastor and Christian education director should maintain an "open door" policy for teachers, consciously offering support and guidance to all who are involved in this crucial ministry.

Growing churches also remain serious about and committed to children's educational programs such as vacation Bible school, summer back yard Bible studies, day care and preschool opportunities. It is difficult (but inspiring) to estimate how many individuals and families have been won into Christian discipleship and local church membership due to such programs. Parents who regularly bring children to pre-school, mothers' morning out or day cares in a local church eventually begin to feel "at home" in the church facility. They are regularly exposed to staff and local church membership. Children are taught principles of Christian living that are then shared back home in the family setting. Banquets and seasonal celebrations periodically draw total family units into the church. Over the course of time, the mere exposure of parents to a church's life through weekday educational programs for children inevitably leads to church growth.

The genuine importance of the program of Christian education in the overall ministry of evangelism and church growth cannot be overestimated. Evangelism and education go hand-in-glove. Often it is within the educational endeavor, within the classroom or small group setting, that the true nature of church is most clearly revealed. Bill Hinson was thus right on target when he wrote: "Each class should strive to be in miniature what they want the church to be as a whole."[4] Where that philosophy is embraced, and where the ministry of Christian education is held in high esteem, growing churches are not hard to find.

A Time For Deciding

Eventually the moment of decision has to come for anyone who has been visiting a church and is considering uniting with it as a member-in-full. Ordinarily that moment is precipitated by an invitation. As Martin Marty observed some time ago: "There is one word that separates growing churches from non-growing churches. That word is 'invite.' "[1] How to extend that invitation in a sincere, encouraging but non-threatening way has long been of interest to persons involved in the ministry of evangelism.

Most denominational and private church-related publishing houses have printed programs training pastors and evangelism committee members regarding the effective mechanics of encouraging prospects to make the move to full membership. Catalogues from such organizations as *Discipleship Resources* (Nashville, Tennessee) and *Net Results* (Lubbock, Texas) provide numerous and interesting alternatives. Particularly helpful are the programs "Reach Out Calling" and "Decision Calls" available from *Net Results*. The point is simply that the programs and tools are out there for the asking. Those who do not ask virtually plan to fail.

One thing appears certain: Winning persons into a permanent relationship with a church is the dual responsibility of laity and clergy. Initially it is understood that most persons attend a church because they are invited by a lay member of the congregation. "In most congregations 83 percent of first-time visitors have been personally invited by a friend, neighbor or relative."[2] Roughly six percent attend first because of the minister. However, when those persons get around to making their final decision about joining the church, few say "yes" without having had some contact/conversation with a staff minister (and the more who have some contact with the senior minister, the higher the percentage of those who join).

At small (averaging less than 85 at worship) to medium sized churches (averaging less than 225 at worship),[3] still the most effective approach seems to be for the pastor to make a house call upon prospective members to secure the decision to join. A bonding takes place when the minister enters the home of the prospect, establishing a personal relationship that goes beyond the merely professional. Most persons seeking membership in small-to-medium sized churches have upon their personal agendas the need to know and be known (by both church members and clergy). Frequently smaller churches are sought out due to persons' acknowledged lack of and need for intimacy. Often those persons find security in knowing that moments of trial or hardship, endured alone in times past, will not have to be faced alone in times yet to come. Thus, there is a special desire to have a personal relationship with a pastor who is both familiar and accessible. Few things facilitate the bonding so much as having the minister visit and appear relaxed and comfortable in the person's home. In churches small-to-medium in size, it is particularly helpful to church growth if the pastor makes a practice of entering the domain of the prospective member with the invitation to become part of the church family.

That luxury is not always afforded to pastors of large and rapidly growing churches. Thus, many of those ministers must find new and creative ways of establishing relationship with prospects "on campus." The adult membership class provides an excellent opportunity. The pastor meets during the Sunday school hour with a pre-determined group of prospective members to lead them in a study of what membership in the church will involve. Over the course of four to six weeks, the pastor thus gets to know the prospective members on a personal basis and they go away feeling that bonding has been established.

A strong program developed at a certain rapidly growing church is called "The Get Acquainted Dinner." The idea received national attention in an issue of *Net Results*. Subsequently numerous churches have put it to the test with almost unanimously positive results. Consider the format (which, of course, may be adapted to suit the needs of the particular church employing it).

The evangelism committee compiles a list of persons who have visited the church more than once within the last three months. To that list is added the names of any long-term prospects who have not yet joined. A theme for an evening meal is selected (seasonal themes are enjoyable — Italian or French sidewalk cafe around Valentine's Day, an outdoor picnic near the fourth of July, pilgrim's potluck near Thanksgiving.) Members of the committee volunteer or enlist the aid of church friends in designing a menu that is tasty but easy to prepare and is in keeping with the theme. (Serve lasagna, salad, bread, beverages and cake for Italian night at Valentine's — or, grilled burgers and hot dogs, baked beans, lemonade and fresh fruit or ice cream for the picnic near the fourth of July). The fellowship hall is decorated in a fashion appropriate to the theme with specific intent that no more than eight persons can be seated at any one table.

Printed invitations are sent to everyone on the prospective members' list (with a reasonable R.S.V.P. date — such as 48 hours prior to the dinner). Announcements are made in the pulpit for three successive Sundays prior to the occasion (thus making certain that those who are not on the list but might be interested in attending are encouraged to come).

On the night of the event, assign various evangelism committee members the responsibility of being "mixers." Some will be stationed at a table at the entrance to the fellowship hall, equipped with name tags for all who attend (make certain that there are ample supplies of name tags and food to accommodate those who come without responding to the R.S.V.P.). Other committee members will be assigned to the fellowship hall, floating from group to group, making certain that no visitor enters the room and is ignored or left alone.

Two members of the committee or church staff members are assigned seats at each table (one on either end at opposite sides). They will spend the meal time chatting with the six prospective members who sit at the table (thus beginning and/or enhancing the visitors' feelings of being connected to the local *ecclesia*).

Following the meal comes a time of introductions. This is done table by table so that each prospective member may be introduced to the gathering at large (individually and as families). Lead questions may be such things as: "What are your names?" "How long have you been in this community?" "What do you do professionally?" "What or who first brought you to our church?" Occasionally someone will feel ill at ease on his feet in front of a group of virtual strangers (though by the end of the meal time everyone should feel comfortable with the others at his table). In the event that a participant would rather not speak, the committee or staff member at that table will assume the privilege of introducing that individual/family to the group at large. This can be done in such fashion that all are made to feel comfortable.

Once introductions have been made and the inevitable light-heartedness of the moment has been enjoyed, the committee chairperson will call upon selected staff members and church officials to make brief, positive remarks on the ministry of the church. It is especially important that persons who coordinate the ministries of children, youth, singles and senior adults take two or three minutes each to highlight what the church does in those important areas. Likewise, someone actively involved in the ministry of education should speak to the wide array of educational opportunities provided by the church (both on Sundays and weekdays/nights). Men's and women's organizations should be represented, as well as all choral groups. Someone representing the missions ministries should briefly address the outreach endeavors in which the church is involved. Last of all, ministerial staff should speak (again briefly) about their areas of responsibility. For example, the director of Christian education can speak to the educational opportunities previously mentioned in this paragraph. The pastor(s) can deal with what church members should expect in worship and in times of personal need. Day care or pre-school directors can take just a moment to highlight the work of their programs. The presentations should be quick, crisp and uniformly upbeat. This is not an occasion for discussing what the church hopes to do better in times to come. It is a time for quickly underscoring as many positive aspects of the church's ministry as possible. The intent is to attract the persons seated at the tables to make the decision to call this church their home.

At the close of the evening, each prospective member is given an envelope. Inside that envelope is a form which they are asked to fill out and hand to one of the staff or committee members on their way out. It is important, therefore, that a staff or committee member is stationed at each exit as the participants begin to file out. The event is designed to bring people to a moment of decision-making. It is an undeniable fact that those who are allowed to take the forms home and think about it will ordinarily put them aside and forget rather than think. Thus, the form should be completed and handed in as they leave the fellowship hall. Consider this sample form *(see page 76)* used at Boone United Methodist Church (Boone, North Carolina).

The bottom line is that some well defined, clear, structured approach to decision solicitation must be in place for a church to grow. New members will not come out of the woodwork in any impressive number when pastors or church members simply sit back and hope that folks know they are welcome. Most of the time the decision requires personal in-house contact by one of the church's ministers. Sometimes, in larger church situations, the adult membership class does suffice. Likewise in growing churches, well organized events (such as the get acquainted dinner) becomes an effective tool for bringing prospective members to the point of making a decision. Churches that find a method that fits their profile are growing churches.

**We hope you will say "yes" to becoming a member
of the Boone United Methodist Church family!**

Please check one of the following lines and provide appropriate information as requested.

_____ Yes, I/We wish to become members of Boone United Methodist Church.

_____ I/We will join by Letter of Transfer from:

_____ Church

address: _____ (street or P.O. Box)

_____, _____, _____
　　　　　(city),　　　　　　　　(state)　　　(zip)

_____ I/We wish to join by first-time Profession of Faith.

I/We have _____, have not _____ been baptized.

The following date will be a convenient time for us to unite with Boone Methodist Church:

December 3 _____ (8:45 service ____; 10:55 service ____)

December 10 _____ (8:45 service ____; 10:55 service ____)

December 17 _____ (8:45 service ____; 10:55 service ____)

December 24 _____ (8:45 service ____; 10:55 service ____)

_____ I/We do not wish to become a member of this church.

Signed: _____

Address: _____

_____

_____, _____, _____
　　　　　(city)　　　　　　　　(state)　　　(zip)

Phone No.: _____-_____-_____

76

Assimilation

The ministry of assimilation is properly the concern of the shepherding task force or the membership care committee, not the responsibility of the evangelism committee. Nonetheless, it is sufficiently important (and sufficiently related to the ministry of evangelism) that brief mention needs to be made.

There is more than ample statistical evidence to prove that individuals who join a church and are not quickly connected to a small group or task force will almost as quickly disappear. Most studies indicate the average activity duration of a non-assimilated new church member is approximately six months. Some with expertise in the field estimate the average duration will be closer to three months. Either way, unless a person is quickly connected to the church family, he will not long remain active in attendance or stewardship. Once fallen through the church cracks, only 15 percent are ever reclaimed into active membership. Thus, the work of assimilation is absolutely indispensable to a church that wants to grow in strength and spirit (as opposed to merely in numbers).

Many authorities in the field of church growth and redevelopment contend that assimilation must begin before a person officially joins the church. Recalling a principle noted in "Prayer Power, Bible Power And Small Group Dynamics," persons often come to church membership via their involvement in scouting, music, study courses or recreational opportunities provided by the congregation. Joining is a natural and easy transition, as the new members had a prior (and important) relationship with the church and already felt a sense of ownership in its program(s). Churches should learn from that lesson as they deal with other individuals who have begun visiting in worship but are not yet involved in any additional relationship with classes or groups sponsored by the congregation.

Evangelism committee members, on the initial visit in a prospective member's home, will discover intresting information about their hosts. The presence of a piano in the den will prompt a question that results in an awareness of a family member's musical abilities. That note should be made on the back of the card that will be returned to the pastor and the committee file. In another home, a resident will mention his athletic background. A similar notation is made on the card. Elsewhere, someone will mention her lifetime involvement with the program of scouting. Write it on the card. The committee chairperson or secretary will read the notations and pass names along to appropriate church leaders (choir directors, softball coaches, scout troop leaders). Simply being aware of a prospective member's interests and abilities significantly facilitates the task of assimilation. Any church will appear far more attractive to a prospect if it offers opportunities for pursuing personal interests and/or putting to use personal skills.

Sunday school is perhaps the primary place where assimilation occurs. It is important that all prospective members be encouraged to attend Sunday school. Therefore, the lay visitation teams should be well versed in the various classes the church offers (including a basic understanding of curriculum plus a personal awareness of who teaches where, age and marital status groupings). Likewise, it is a definite plus if the printed material the visitors take into the homes of prospects has clear (and impressive) data about the entire ministry of Christian education. As noted before, the Sunday school is a wonderful place for making the transition from "congregation" to "fellowship." Once that transition has been made, assimilation is achieved.

Bill Hinson reports on the philosophy and success of this approach in his large downtown Houston church:

> *"We must be diligent in assimilating all new members. Since we have begun . . . assimilating people into Sunday school classes and Bible study groups before their enrollment in the church, I have discovered that the problems of assimilation have decreased dramatically."* [1]

Assimilation and stewardship are united in a happy marriage through the simple tool of the new member packet (distributed to each person uniting with a church at the time he is publicly accepted). Most include a certificate of membership plus printed information about the local church (similar or identical to that which is taken to prospective members' homes on the initial visit), printed information about the denomination and its basic beliefs, a financial commitment card, printed information about men's, women's and youth groups and a talent/personal interest survey form. This provides the new member with an opportunity to express his desires to be of service to the church. The data is easily filed via computer or a simple alphabetized file cabinet. Work area chairpersons are encouraged to consult the file when selecting members of their committee and task forces. Pastors and other staff regularly peruse the materials with a keen eye out for involving new persons in the ongoing ministry of the congregation. The membership care committee monitors the process to make certain that no one is lost in the shuffle, but that all persons' responses are taken seriously and employed faithfully where humanly possible.

The following forms[2] are examples of how two churches approach this task. Each congregation, of course, will need to design an instrument unique to its own program. Likewise, each will need to assign some very dependable individual the role of volunteer coordinator. Not to develop a form and format is to posture the congregation to fail in the work of assimilation. Note that one form is specifically designed for use on a church computer data base, while the other (though adaptable to computer) can be easily stored and used in an ordinary filing cabinet.

Through God's help, I will commit myself to do his work through _____(name of church)_____ by volunteering for:

ADMINISTRATIVE

Male   **Female**

( )   1 ( ) ABO Office Volunteer
( )   2 ( ) ABS Safety/Bus Committee
( )   3 ( ) ABD Bus/Van Driver
( )   4 ( ) ABB Bulletin Board 1x/mo
( )   5 ( ) ABC Calligraphy
( )   6 ( ) ABI Computer Data Input

AGE LEVEL MINISTRIES

Nursery Ministries

( )   7 ( ) BNC Serve as Captain/Co-Captain
( )   8 ( ) BNA Nursery 1x/mo 8:30
( )   9 ( ) BNB Nursery 1x/mo 9:40
( )   10 ( ) BND Nursery 1x/mo 11:00
( )   11 ( ) BNN Nursery 1x/mo 6:30 p.m.
( )   12 ( ) BNW Nursery 1x/mo 6:45 (Wed)
( )   13 ( ) BTS Teach 2-yr. Sunday School, 9:40
( )   14 ( ) BTD Teach 2-yr. Sunday School, 11:00
( )   15 ( ) BSB Substitute Teacher 2-yr. Sunday School, 9:40
( )   16 ( ) BSC Substitute Teacher 2-yr. Sunday School, 11:00
( )   17 ( ) BVC Visit New Mothers/Cradle Roll
( )   18 ( ) BDL Deliver Rose/Bibles/Yard Signs
( )   19 ( ) BFF Friends for Life

Children's Ministries

( )   20 ( ) KTS Teach Sunday School
( )   21 ( ) KAS Assist in Sunday School
( )   22 ( ) KSS Substitute in Sunday School
( )   23 ( ) KHP Help/Child. Church-Preschool
( )   24 ( ) KHE Help in Child. Church-Elementary
( )   25 ( ) KHH Assist in Handicapped Class
( )   26 ( ) KSE Summer Events
( )   27 ( ) KVT Vacation Bible School
( )   28 ( ) MD3 Children's Choir-Director/Helper
( )   29 ( ) MKC Children's Choir Pianist
( )   30 ( ) KP9 Puppet Ministry
( )   31 ( ) KC9 Clown Ministry
( )   32 ( ) KDC Help in Day Camp (local)
( )   33 ( ) KBL Help in Elementary Camp-Blue Lake
( )   34 ( ) KRF Rainbow Facilitator

Youth Ministries

( )   35 ( ) YAB Teach in Sunday School
( )   36 ( ) YAC Assist in Sunday School

Male   Female
( )   37 ( ) YAA Christmas Tree Sales
( )   38 ( ) YAD Serve UMYF Snack Suppers
( )   39 ( ) YAE Help w/Work Project
( )   40 ( ) YAF Transportation for Work Project
( )   41 ( ) YAG Have Afterglow on Sunday night
( )   42 ( ) YAH Covenant Group Leader
( )   43 ( ) YAI Jr. High Wednesday Bible Study
( )   44 ( ) MPT Youth Choir-Parent Team

College Ministries
( )   45 ( ) JSS Substitute in Sunday School
( )   46 ( ) JHL Host Late Night 1x/Summer
( )   47 ( ) JUS Lead Under-Shepherd Group

Adult Ministries
( )   48 ( ) RTS Teach Sunday School
( )   49 ( ) RE9 Easter Egg Hunt

Older Adult Ministries
( )   50 ( ) ROQ Transport - 3rd & 4th Thursday
( )   51 ( ) ROT Teach Crafts - 4th Thursday
( )   52 ( ) ROA Help w/Friends - 3rd Thursday
( )   53 ( ) RO4 Help w/4th Thursday

Family Ministries
( )   54 ( ) RS9 Spring Festival
( )   55 ( ) RF9 Fall Festival
( )   56 ( ) RX9 Special Events

WORK AREAS
Church and Society
( )   57 ( ) PBD Blood Donor
( )   58 ( ) PB9 Blood Drive Worker
( )   59 ( ) PP8 Prison Ministry
( )   60 ( ) PA9 Substance Abuse Ministry
( )   61 ( ) PVS Victims Support Ministry
( )   62 ( ) PFC Family Issues/Concerns

Congregational Care
( )   63 ( ) LV9 Lay Minister Program
( )   64 ( ) CH9 Hospital Ministry
( )   65 ( ) CV9 Shut-in Ministry
( )   66 ( ) CU9 Nursing Home Ministry
( )   67 ( ) CG9 Grief Crisis Support
( )   68 ( ) CF9 Flower Delivery (Hospitals)
( )   69 ( ) CPW PAWS (Pets Are Working Saints)

Educational

Male   **Female**

( )   70 ( ) HSA Sunday School Secretary 8:30
( )   71 ( ) HSB Sunday School Secretary 9:40
( )   72 ( ) HSC Sunday School Secretary 11:00
( )   73 ( ) HL9 Library Committee

Ethnic Minority

( )   74 ( ) IS9 Special Projects
( )   75 ( ) IA9 Adult Literacy

Evangelism

( )   76 ( ) ENV Neighborhood Visitation
( )   77 ( ) EAR Attendance Registration
( )   78 ( ) ETC Telephone Committee
( )   79 ( ) ERF Records/Filing. Monday-Wednesday, a.m.
( )   80 ( ) EMP New Member Photography
( )   81 ( ) EPM Prayer Ministry

Food Service

( )   82 ( ) F19 Sunday Breakfast 1x/mo
( )   83 ( ) F29 Snack Supper 1x/mo
( )   84 ( ) F59 Wednesday Night Supper 1x/mo
( )   85 ( ) FN9 Noon Salad Luncheon
( )   86 ( ) 4th Thursday/Friends
( )   87 ( ) FP9 Hospitality

Health and Welfare

( )   88 ( ) Q59 Selma Children's Home
( )   89 ( ) QA9 Angel Tree Christmas Program

Leisure Ministries

( )   90 ( ) GCL Coach Ladies' Softball
( )   91 ( ) GCM Coach Men's Softball
( )   92 ( ) GCY Coach Youth Softball
( )   93 ( ) GCB Coach Men's Basketball
( )   94 ( ) GYB Coach Youth Basketball
( )   95 ( ) GLE Lead Exercise Program
( )   96 ( ) GSB Boy Scouts
( )   97 ( ) GSC Cub Scouts

Missions-In Christ's Way

( )   98 ( ) SA9 Spiritual Follow-up
( )   99 ( ) SB9 Professional/Work Skills
( )   100 ( ) SC9 Financial Counseling
( )   101 ( ) SD9 Christian Job Exchange
( )   102 ( ) SE9 Food Pantry
( )   103 ( ) SF9 Clothes Closet

Missions-Local

Male   Female

( )   104 ( ) SG9 Sav-A-Life
( )   105 ( ) SH9 Meals on Wheels
( )   106 ( ) SI9 WLBF Radio
( )   107 ( ) SJ9 S.T.E.P.
( )   108 ( ) SSS Bell Street-Sunday Afternoon
( )   109 ( ) SVB Bell Street-Vacation Bible School

Missions-World and National

( )   110 ( ) SK9 World and National Outreach
( )   111 ( ) SL9 Serve on a Work Team
( )   112 ( ) SM9 Serve on a Medical Team
( )   113 ( ) SN9 Pray for Missionary
( )   114 ( ) SO9 Correspond with Missionary
( )   115 ( ) SP9 House Missionaries
( )   116 ( ) SQ9 $10 Club

Music

( )   117 ( ) MZ3 Adult Choir-Morning
( )   118 ( ) MQ3 Adult Choir-Evening
( )   119 ( ) MBH Adult Handbells
( )   120 ( ) MO3 Instrument Ensembles
( )   121 ( ) MK3 Pianist
( )   122 ( ) MTS Maintain Sound System
( )   123 ( ) MTC Tape Ministry/Clerical

Newspaper Ministry

( )   124 ( ) NW9 Writers
( )   125 ( ) NE9 Editors and Proofreaders
( )   126 ( ) NG9 Graphic Arts
( )   127 ( ) NP9 Still Photography

Religious Drama

( )   128 ( ) DDA Acting-Directing
( )   129 ( ) DDC Costumes
( )   130 ( ) DDM Make-up
( )   131 ( ) DDL Spotlight
( )   132 ( ) DDS Scenery

Stewardship

( )   133 ( ) XRA Lay Reader 8:30
( )   134 ( ) XRB Lay Reader 9:40
( )   135 ( ) XRC Lay Reader 11:00
( )   136 ( ) XNM New Member Orientation
( )   137 ( ) XNP New Member Packets
( )   138 ( ) XLI Lay Involvement Coordination

Worship

Male   Female

( )   139 ( ) UW9 Member UMW Circle
( )   140 ( ) UCI Interested in UMW Circle

United Methodist Men

( )   141 ( ) UM9 Interested in UMM

Worship

( )   142 ( ) WA3 Sanctuary Usher 1x/mo 8:30
( )   143 ( ) WB3 Sanctuary Usher 1x/mo 9:40
( )   144 ( ) WC3 Sanctuary Usher 1x/mo 11:00
( )   145 ( ) WMA Sanctuary Usher 1x/mo 7:00 p.m.
( )   146 ( ) WDI Parking Usher 1x/mo
( )   147 ( ) WEA Communion Usher
( )   148 ( ) WFA Communion Server 8:30
( )   149 ( ) WFB Communion Server 9:40
( )   150 ( ) WFC Communion Server 11:00
( )   151 ( ) WGP Communion Preparation
( )   152 ( ) WJ3 Greeter 1x/mo 8:30
( )   153 ( ) WK3 Greeter 1x/mo 9:40
( )   154 ( ) WL3 Greeter 1x/mo 11:00
( )   155 ( ) WH9 Count Attendance
( )   156 ( ) WI9 Acolyte Coordinator

Worship Support Area

( )   157 ( ) ZD9 Special Decorations
( )   158 ( ) ZC9 Sanctuary Care
( )   159 ( ) ZA Altar Care

Miscellaneous

( )   160 ( ) OWN Wherever the Church needs me
( )   161 ( ) OTR Other (Specify)

_____

_____

Name _____
                        (Please Print)

Telephone _____

Respond to this Call into Meaningful Service at
__(place name of church here)__ Church

Name _____

Address _____

_____

Phone (Home)_____ (work)_____

Status: _____ Member _____ Associate Member _____ Visitor

Date: _____/_____/_____ Birthdate: _____/_____/_____

I believe in the mission of (insert name) Church of (city, state). As we plan to serve the needs of the members of this congregation, and of the community and the world in which we live, I respond to these opportunities for Meaningful Service and would like to serve my church in the following areas:

Education	Am Doing	Willing To Do
Bible Study Leader	_____	_____
Sunday School Teacher		
Children	_____	_____
Youth	_____	_____
Adult	_____	_____
Assistant/Substitute Teacher	_____	_____
Sunday School Superintendent	_____	_____
Sunday School Secretary	_____	_____
Children's Church	_____	_____
Preschool Substitute	_____	_____
Prepare Youth Suppers	_____	_____
Counselor - UMKIDS	_____	_____
Counselor - UMYF	_____	_____
Media Resource	_____	_____
Cradle Roll Worker	_____	_____
Nursery Worker	_____	_____
Vacation Bible School		
Coordinator	_____	_____
Teacher	_____	_____
Assistant Teacher	_____	_____
WORSHIP		
Acolyte (Candlelighter)	_____	_____
Acolyte Coordinator	_____	_____
Acolyte Parent	_____	_____
Altar Guild	_____	_____

85

	Am Doing	Willing To Do
Communion Steward	_____	_____
Lay Speaker	_____	_____
Usher 8:45 Service	_____	_____
Usher 10:55 Service	_____	_____
Greeter 8:45 Service	_____	_____
Greeter 10:55 Service	_____	_____

Stewardship

Pledge Campaign Vol.	_____	_____
Church Teller	_____	_____
Record Church Attendance	_____	_____
Communion Steward	_____	_____
Special Offerings Volunteer	_____	_____
Rice Bowl Volunteer	_____	_____

Music

Chancel Choir (10:55)	_____	_____
Chancel Choir (8:45)	_____	_____
Cherub Choir (Preschool)	_____	_____
Children's Choir (K-2)	_____	_____
Bell Choirs (Children/Adult)	_____	_____
Instrumentalist	_____	_____
Specify:_____		
Soloist	_____	_____
Organist Substitute	_____	_____
Pianist	_____	_____
Methodist/Pres. Choir (3-7)	_____	_____
Youth Choir (8-12)	_____	_____

Social Ministry

Children's Summer Program	_____	_____
Hunger Coalition	_____	_____
Youth Network Volunteer	_____	_____
Habitat for Humanity	_____	_____
Hospitality House	_____	_____

Council on Minstries Work Areas

Education	_____	_____
Evangelism	_____	_____
Worship	_____	_____
Stewardship	_____	_____
Missions	_____	_____
Volunteer Ministries	_____	_____
Kitchen Committee	_____	_____
Higher Education/Ministry	_____	_____
Christian Unity &		
Interreligious Concerns	_____	_____

	Am Doing	Willing To Do
Church and Society	_____	_____
Religion and Race	_____	_____
Membership Care Committee	_____	_____
Health & Welfare Rep.	_____	_____
Role & Status of Women	_____	_____
Scout Representative	_____	_____
Family Life Committee	_____	_____
Preschool Coordinator	_____	_____
Elementary Coordinator	_____	_____
Children's Council	_____	_____
Youth Coordinator		
Youth Council	_____	_____
Adult Coordinator	_____	_____
Adult Council	_____	_____

Organizations

	Am Doing	Willing To Do
United Methodist Men	_____	_____
United Methodist Women	_____	_____
Youth Fellowship (UMYF)	_____	_____
Elem. Fellowship (UMKIDS)	_____	_____
Singles Fellowship (SOS)	_____	_____
Scouts: Specify _____	_____	_____
XYZ (Seniors Group, Age 50+)	_____	_____
Wesley Foundation	_____	_____
Disciples Bible Study	_____	_____
Shepherding Care Program	_____	_____
Sunday Breakfast Hosts	_____	_____

What Skills Would You Have To Share?

_____ Typing
_____ Mailings
_____ General Office
_____ Telephone
_____ Office machines
_____ Computer Skills
_____ Audio/Video Recording
_____ Photography
_____ Posters/Signs
_____ Art Work
_____ Calligraphy
_____ Publicity
_____ Public Relations
_____ Babysitting/Nursery Care
_____ Writing/Editing
_____ Public/Speaking
_____ Discussion leader

_____ Counselor/Consultant
     _____ Legal
     _____ Medical/Dental
     _____ Financial
     _____ Computer
     _____ Insurance/Medicare
_____ Estate Planning
_____ Parking Lot Attendant
_____ Electronics
_____ Cooking/Baking
_____ Calling/Visiting
_____ Cultural Events
        _____ Entertainment
        Specify: _____
_____ Interior Decorating
_____ Furniture Repair
_____ Sewing
_____ Shopping/Errands
_____ Arrange Flowers
_____ Dancing
_____ Yard Work
_____ Landscape/Planting
_____ Painting/Papering
_____ Wood Working
_____ Crafts
_____ Electrical
_____ Plumbing
_____ Carpentry
_____ Heating/Air Conditioning
_____ Brick/Concrete
_____ Wash Windows
_____ Phoning/Coordinating
_____ Tutoring

Other: _____

_____

_____

_____

_____

_____

_____

_____

What agencies, boards, committees of the District or Conference do you serve on?

_____

_____

_____

Please list your volunteer activities in the community: _____

_____

_____

Occupation (present or retired from): _____

Wedding Date: _____/_____/_____

I usually attend: _____ 8:45 Service _____ 10:55, and the

_____Sunday School Class.

Do you need transportation to church events?

_____ no

_____ sometimes

_____ often

Please list the following information for others in your home:

Name	Birthday	Relationship	Age

Signature _____

Getting Started

Herb Miller frequently tells his audience not to confuse the study of evangelism with the doing of evangelism.[1] That temptation is too easily embraced. Perhaps Koheleth had met with the wrong type evangelism committee and thus was prompted to observe: ". . . much study is a weariness of the flesh (Ecclesiastes 12:12)." Evangelism committees should meet to serve, not merely to study. Any investigation of this material or any "how to" guide book should be simply an impetus to get up, get out and get going. It is through personal contact with prospective members that the success of the program will ultimately be attained.

Here are a few clues about getting started.

1 — Do not invest the local church's nominating committee with the authority to select membership on the evangelism/visitation committee. To do so is to build into the system an immediate disadvantage. Nominating committees are notorious for placing into consideration for any posts the names of personal friends. Thus, Aunt Harriet's name will inevitably come up because niece Jane is on the committee. And though Aunt Harriet is emminently skilled for a post on the altar guild, her skills (and interests) in visitation evangelism may be virtually non-existent. Carl's long-time friend and partner in the men's Bible club, Ernest, is also placed into nomination. Ernest may have immeasurable abilities for the work of the trustees or finance committee, but his social skills and graces may be next to nonexistent. Nonetheless, through a congregational buddy system, a nominating committee may put together an evangelism task force that is particularly ill suited for the work.

2 — Leave the assignment of evangelism committee membership to the pastor(s) or the pastor(s) and committee chairperson. They know best which persons in the congregation are uniquely able to bring needed strengths to the evangelistic task.

91

3 — Prospective members of the committee should be contacted in person by the pastor (preferably along with committee chairperson) and impressed with the significance of the task. Special mention should be made of why the person was chosen, so that membership on the committee is seen as an honor.

4 — Install committee members during a special evangelism celebration during Sunday morning worship.

5 — Plan two meetings within the first month for discussion of the nature and mission of the local church as well as where it currently is and where the selected leadership wants it to go. The following documents are important pieces of training equipment as the committee members evaluate the strengths and future needs of the congregation they have been called to serve. These documents (or others like them) should be distributed at the first meeting with instructions that they be returned at the second meeting. Discussion of results forms the basis of the first half of the second meeting.[2] *(see pages 94-100)*

6 — Secure video-recording training tape for visitation evangelism. Most denominational publishing houses have ample selections from which to choose. The point is finding one that stimulates the committee membership to do what it has been selected to do.

7 — Select two person visitation teams who are obviously compatible and who will enjoy working together.There is an advantage to sending out husband-wife teams, but it is by no means required. (One note to keep in mind — the visitors you send out should be persons you would enjoy having drop by to visit in your home. They are your hospitality representatives to the target community.)

8 — As indicated earlier, continued publication of committee activities should appear in the church newsletter. Include monthly front page information about new members received (including names, brief personal information, addresses).

9 — Plan Membership Celebration Sundays when uniting with the church can be encouraged. Many persons given to

timidity about standing alone before a congregation find it much easier to join a church when they are enabled to stand with a group. The first Sunday in Advent or Lent is an attractive time for receiving groups into membership. Pentecost Sunday is a natural. Membership Celebration days can be planned on occasions when large attendance is traditional, such as Palm Sunday or Homecoming. Make a good deal of the occasion. Give each new member on these days a carnation to wear. Have evangelism committee members stand with them as hosts or sponsors. Ask the chairperson of the committee to make brief, welcoming remarks from the pulpit (remembering to encourage others present that day who are considering church membership to talk with him before leaving). Membership Celebration days are wonderful motivational vehicles for encouraging the ''almost-readies'' to come to a point of decision.

10 — Undergird the effort with prayer. Evangelism is not our work for the church. Evangelism is God's work through us. Growing churches remember why they are doing what they do and whose work they are about. Keep the efforts theocentric by remaining diligent in prayer.

How Do We Treat First-time Visitors?

	Yes	No
Do we provide visitors parking spaces?	____	____
Do we have a team of greeters for Sunday school and worship?	____	____
Do greeters provide directions, and are directions signs/floor plans posted?	____	____
Are visitors provided with the opportunity/encouragement to sign registration pads and/or visitors' cards?	____	____
Is there a time within the morning worship for church members to meet and welcome visitors?	____	____
Are visitors provided with written information about the church prior to leaving?	____	____
Is there an opportunity for the visitor to have at least a momentary encounter with the pastor?	____	____
Are visitors invited to a Sunday school and/or membership orientation class?	____	____
Are members of the evangelism work team visible and involved in the morning worship service?	____	____
Do the laity provide quick follow-up on first-time visitors (preferably within 36 hours)?	____	____
Are accurate records kept about first-time visitors, and are such records quickly forwarded to the pastor and chairperson of the evangelism team?	____	____

Dreams And Visions Survey Form

Dreaming Dreams and Seeing Visions — In the Local Church

1 — Membership Goals

Current Membership of our church is: _____

By 1994, our membership should be: _____

By 1997, our membership should be: _____

By 2000, our membership should be: _____

2 — Attendance Goals

Current avg. attendance at worship: _____

    Enter by services: _____)

                    (_____)

                    (_____)

By 1994, our avg. attendance should be: _____

    (by services: _____, _____, _____)

By 1997, avg. attendance should be: _____

By 2000, avg. attendance should be: _____

Current avg. attendance at Sunday School: _____

By 1994 avg. attendance at S.S. should be: _____

By 1997 avg. attendance at S.S. should be: _____

By 2000 avg. attendance at S.S. should be: _____

3 — Reaching Persons For Christ

No. Professions of Faith last year: _____

By 1994, desired no. annually: _____

By 1997, desired no. annually: _____

By 2000, desired no. annually: _____

4 — Ministry To Children And Youth

List current programs for children/youth:

Others needed currently:

Projected children's youth needs by year 2000:

5 — Age Level Ministries

What current programs are provided for?

Young adult families.

Singles.

Divorced/widowed.

Senior adults.

Persons with handicapping conditions.

Persons who work Sundays.

What programs might be needed currently?

What additional needs should be addressed by 2000?

6 — Mission Ministries

Current Mission/Social Outreach Ministries:

Current human needs being left unaddressed:

What human needs/mission ministries will present themselves as concerns for local church ministry by the year 2000?

7 — Pastoral Outreach

Current full-time staff positions (by position):

Current part-time staff positions (by position):

Projected additional staff needs:
by 1994:

by 1997:

by 2000:

What measures are being taken/should be taken to encourage persons to consider a profession in full-time ministry?

What three specific areas do you think are currently most closely identified with your church's ministry?

What additions/deletions should be made to that list as we approach the 21st century?

8 — Worship

Number and times of current worship services:

Are all worship services conducted on Sundays?
            Yes _____   No _____
(If alternative days, circle: M   T   W   Th   F   S)

By 1994, how many worship services per week will be needed to meet worship needs? _____

At what hour(s) on Sunday?_____

Will alternative services be needed on days other than Sunday? _____

List current numbers/types of choirs:

Are other choirs needed to meet worship needs? (List)

Does the ministry of music meet the needs of the congregation? (Comment)

How might the ministry of music better meet congregational needs?

Current strengths of worship program: (List)

How could the current worship program be strengthened?

Does your church use the new *(denominational title)* hymnal?
            Yes _____   No _____

98

9 — Christian Education

List current programs of Christian education in addition to Sunday school:

How many ongoing Bible study programs should your church offer to provide adequate spiritual nurture for current membership?

Does your church offer cottage study programs?
Yes _____ No _____

Are any age levels/marital status groups/etc., currently overlooked by your Sunday school or overall Christian education program?

What resources (financial, facility, personnel) would be required to begin effective ministry to those groups?

What new ventures in Christian education should be established by:
1994:

1997:

2000:

10 — Facility

In which areas is your church facility adequate as you face a coming decade?

In which areas are growth/expansion/renovation needed?

Prioritize the needs listed immediately above:

What is required to begin addressing those needs immediately?

What will be the short-term results if these needs are left unaddressed?

What will be the long-term results if those needs are left unaddressed?

11 — Personal Agenda

Looking at the life of your church, what things seem most urgent as you face the future?

What do you think God has in mind for your church in the closing decade of this century?

Postscript

Your church can grow, probably to a greater degree in a more modest amount of time than anyone may concede possible. The only "miracles" required are faith that is stronger than doubts and a commitment to hard work. With those resources at your disposal, your church can grow.

Biblically we are assured that new life can be breathed into all valleys of dry bones and that God desires such. We are not called to work the miracle. We are simply called to enter into partnership with the One who can.

By developing:

- a vision of what your church was created to be and can be,
- a sense of the constituency within your reach,
- a sense of the mission God has entrusted to your congregation regarding that constituency,
- a sensitivity to human need (spiritual as well as physical),
- a faith that Pentecost is as much a contemporary experience as an historical event,
- a trained and devoted team of "workers in the vineyard (Matthew 9:38),"
- a systematic approach to evangelism that embraces competent ministry to all age levels and to the endeavor of Christian education,
- a specific intentionality that prospective members will be assimilated into full church family membership,
- and an unshakeable faith that God is in the midst of all you do and all you are,

Your Church Can Grow!

May God bless you in the adventure of local church evangelism and redevelopment. May your dreams and visions be consistent with God's. May your work be experienced as joy. And may your future be as bright and beautiful as is the love that Christ feels for your church.

Endnotes

The Approach
1. Leslie Weatherhead, "The Real Thing" (sermon on tape, Waco, Texas: Word Publishers, *Twenty Centuries of Great Preaching* series, 1971).

The Need For A Vital Ministry Of Evangelism
1. Donald McGavran, "Beyond the Maintenance of Ministry," *Christianity Today* (Carol Stream, Illinois: Christianity Today Publishers, February 3, 1989).
2. *Ibid.*
3. William H. Willimon and Robert L. Wilson, *Rekindling The Flame* (Nashville: Abingdon Press, 1987), p. 22.
4. Herb Miller, *How To Build A Magnetic Church,* (Nashville: Abingdon Press, 1987), p. 22.
5. *Ibid.*, p. 21.
6. Statistics gathered from Richard B. Wilke, *And Are We Yet Alive?* (Nashville: Abingdon Press, 1986).
7. *Op. Cit.,* Willimon and Wilson, p. 21.

Some Biblical Foundations For Doing Evangelism
1. John Ed Mathison, lecture on "Growth PLUS" training video (Nashville: *Discipleship Resources,* 1987).
2. Herb Miller, *Evangelism's Open Secrets* (St. Louis, Mo.: CBP Press, 1989) p. 29.)

Prayer Power, Bible Power And Small Group Dynamics
1. Arthur Caliandro, lecture at the FCL School of Practical Christianity (Pawling, New York, October, 1989).
2. Harry Denman, speech delivered to Durham District Evangelism Rally (Durham, North Carolina, District of The United Methodist Church, 1972).
3. Paula D'Arcy, lecture at the FCL School of Practical Christianity (Pawling, New York, October, 1989).

4. Information on Wesley and the Bible taken from Evelyn Laycock and James Holsinger, *Awaken The Giant* (Nashville: Abingdon Press, 1989), p. 65.

5. *Op. Cit.*, Miller, *Evangelism's Open Secrets,* p. 45.

Making It Work In The Local Church

1. *Op. Cit.,* Miller *(Evangelism's Open Secrets),* p. 117.

2. *Op. Cit.,* Willimon and Wilson, p. 123.

3. *Op. Cit.,* Wilke, pp. 120-21.

4. *Op. Cit.,* Willimon and Wilson, p. 42.

5. Joe Harding, *Have I Told You Lately?* (Nashville: Church Growth Press, 1989), p. 15.

6. *Op. Cit.,* Willimon and Wilson, p. 111.

7. John Killinger, *Fundamentals Of Preaching* (Nashville: Abingdon Press, 1985), p. 189.

8. "Seven Characteristics of a Growing Church," *Church Administration* (October, 1975), p. 7.

9. *Op. Cit.,* Killinger, p. 14.

10. *Op. Cit.,* Willimon and Wilson, p. 112.

11. *Op. Cit.,* Killinger, pp. 23, 25.

12. *Op. Cit.,* Willimon and Wilson, p. 23.

13. *Op. Cit.,* Laycock and Holsinger, p. 79.

14. Walter Underwood, *Being Human, Being Hopeful* (Nashville: Abingdon Press, 1987), p. 44.

15. Edgar Jackson, *How To Preach To People's Needs* (Grand Rapids, Mich.: Baker Book House, 1974), pp. 13-14.

16. "A Conversation with Norman Vincent and Ruth Peale," recorded at the FCL School of Practical Christianity (Pawling, New York, October, 1989).

17. John Sutherland Bonnell, "Preaching" (lecture delivered to clergy conference at Mannasset, Virginia).

18. *Op. Cit.,* Killinger, p. 163.

19. Leonard Sweet, keynote address, "1990 Finch Lectures on Preaching" (Greensboro, North Carolina, 1990).

20. *Op. Cit.,* Harding, p. 17.

21. *Op. Cit.,* Killinger, pp. 10, 13.

22. *Op. Cit.,* Laycock and Holsinger, p. 33.

23. *Ibid.*, p. 36.

24. *Op. Cit.*, D'Arcy (lecture).

25. "A Time To Seek," *Newsweek* (New York: Newsweek, Inc., December 17, 1990), p. 51.

26. *Op. Cit.*, Miller, *Evangelism's Open Secrets,* p. 64.

27. *Ibid.*, p. 17.

28. See "FRANGELISM" model brochures prepared by *Discipleship Resources* (Nashville, Tennessee).

29. *Op. Cit.*, Miller, *Evangelism's Open Secrets,* p. 50.

30. Joe Harding and Ralph Mohney, *Vision 2000* (Nashville: *Discipleship Resources,*1991), p. 86.

The Serious Business Of Worship

1. Ralph and Nell Mohney, *Churches of Vision* (Nashville: *Discipleship Resources,*1990).

2. Lewis Grizzard, "Listen, see why church attendance is off," from *The Atlanta Constitution*, August, 1990.

Christian Education

1. *Op. Cit.*, Laycock and Holsinger, p. 24.

2. *Ibid.*, p. 99.

3. Warren Hartman, *Five Audiences* (Nashville: Abingdon Press, 1987), pp. 79-80.

4. William Hinson, *A Place To Dig In,* (Nashville: Abingdon Press, 1987), pp. 79-80.

A Time For Deciding

1. Martin Marty, quoted in issue of *Context* magazine, 1984.

2. *Op. Cit.*, Harding and Mohney, p. 86.

3. Lyle Schaller, *Growing Plans* (Nashville: Abingdon Press, 1983), pp. 54-55.

Assimilation

1. *Op. Cit.,* Hinson, p. 122.

2. Membership talent/interest forms from Fraser Memorial United Methodist Church, Montgomery, Alabama and Boone United Methodist Church, Boone, North Carolina.

Getting Started

1. From "Person Involved in Evangelism" training script (Lubbock, Texas: The National Evangelistic Association).

2. James Cowell, *Extending Your Congregation's Welcome* (Nashville: *Discipleship Resources,*1989), p. 18.